CAPITALISM
COMMUNISM
&
COWISM

A NEW ECONOMICS
FOR THE 21ST CENTURY

By
Dr. Sahadeva dasa

B.com., FCA., AICWA., PhD
Chartered Accountant

Soul Science University Press
www.cowism.com

Readers interested in the subject matter of this
book are invited to correspond with the publisher at:
SoulScienceUniversity@gmail.com +91 98490 95990

First Edition: October 2011

Soul Science University Press expresses its gratitude to the Bhaktivedanta Book
Trust International (BBT), for the use of quotes by His Divine Grace
A.C.Bhaktivedanta Swami Prabhupada.
Copyright Bhaktivedanta Book Trust International (BBT)

ISBN 978-81-909760-6-0

Published by:
Dr. Sahadeva dasa for Soul Science University Press

Website by :
E. Karnika Yashwant (Ens.org.in)

Printed by:
Rainbow Print Pack, Hyderabad

To order a copy write to chandra@rgbooks.co.in
or buy online: at www.rgbooks.co.in

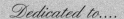
Dedicated to....
His Divine Grace A.C.Bhaktivedanta Swami Prabhupada

"Human society needs only sufficient grain and sufficient cows to solve its economic problems. All other things but these two are artificial necessities created by man to kill his valuable life at the human level and waste his time in things which are not needed."
~Srila Prabhupada
(Srimad Bhagavatam 3.2.29)

By The Same Author
Oil-Final Countdown To A Global Crisis And Its Solutions
End of Modern Civilization And Alternative Future
To Kill Cow Means To End Human Civilization
Cow And Humanity - Made For Each Other
Cows Are Cool - Love 'Em!
Wondrous Glories of Vraja
(More information on availability at the back)

Contents

Preface

.

The world is in search of an economic system that works for the people and the Planet. And this search has been going on for the last one hundred years without much success.

Industrial revolution started with capitalism but the communist revolution overthrew it in many places. Socialism was proposed as a viable alternative but it collapsed before too long. Capitalism in its various forms and shapes is still running but every now and then it runs into serious difficulties. One such difficulty has come in the form of U.S. credit downgrade.

Endless debate is going on whether S&P, the rating agency, was justified in stripping America of its AAA rating and — adding insult to injury — even attaching a negative outlook to the new AA+ rating. But this historic action has now taken place, and the global system must adjust. There are consequences and there will be uncertainties.

Not so long ago, it was deemed unthinkable that America could lose its AAA. Indeed, "risk free" and "US Treasuries" were interchangeable terms — so much so that the global financial system was constructed, and has operated on the assumption that America's AAA was a constant at the core, and not a variable. But this notion has been proven wrong.

So what is the solution when nothing seems to be working? To search out a suitable economic system we need not go very far. We just have to look back in our not so distant past. For thousands of years, humanity has been sustained by an economic system which was in perfect harmony with our environment, internal and external. This model was based on land, domesticated animals and other gifts of nature. This was a completely localized, decentralized, self-sufficient and nature dependent model, based on the concept of 'plain living and high thinking'.

We may like it or not, but our time and options are running out. Our present economic paradigms are leading us fast on the path of self-annihilation.

Dr Sahadeva dasa

Sahadeva dasa

1st October 2011
Secunderabad, India

Section-I

Economics
Techno-Industrial

1.

Economics

One Of The Basic Institutions

Economics is a social science that examines the financial behavior of human beings. It analyzes the production, distribution, and consumption of goods and services. The term economics comes from the Greek word 'oikonomia', which basically means 'management or administration of a household'.

Lionel Robbins in 1932, set out the classic brief definition of economics as 'the science which studies human behavior as a relation between scarce means having alternative uses.' Without scarcity and alternative uses, there is no economic problem.

Economics as a separate discipline, in its modern form, emerged after the publication of Adam Smith's 'The Wealth of Nations' in 1776. The book identified land, labor, and capital as the three factors of production and the major contributors to a nation's wealth.

Economics has two broad branches: microeconomics, where the unit of analysis is the individual agent, such as a household or firm, and macroeconomics, where the unit of analysis is an economy as a whole. Macroeconomics addresses issues affecting an entire economy like unemployment, inflation, economic growth, and monetary and fiscal policy. Microeconomics confines itself to the behavior of basic elements in the economy, including individual markets and agents (such as consumers and firms, buyers and sellers). Other distinctions include: between positive economics (describing 'what is') and normative economics (advocating 'what ought to be').

A Nobel Prize is offered in economics for advancements in research. No other social science is awarded its own Nobel Prize. The expanding domain of economics in the social sciences has been described as economic imperialism.

Economics aims to explain how economies work and how economic agents interact. Economic analysis is applied throughout society, not  only in business, finance and government, but also in crime, education, the family, health, law, politics, religion, social institutions, war, and science. Economics is a very important field of human activity and it has impact on all these aforesaid social fields. If we have got our economics right, everything else is right and if the economics is wrong, everything else goes wrong.

This explains, at least partially, as to why the human society is in a mess today in spite of considerable advances made in the fields of science, technology and commerce. Something is just not right with the ways we make our money, the way we keep it and the way we spend it.

"It is well enough that people of the nation do not understand our banking and monetary system, for if they did, I believe there would be a revolution before tomorrow morning." – Henry Ford

2.
McDonaldization And Cocacolonization
Of The World Economy

Modern Economic Model Is All Western

At present the economics that we are acquainted with is a Western one. When talking of economics or matters pertaining to it, we use a Western vocabulary and we think within the conceptual framework of Western economic theory.

Well, its not just economics! Since last few centuries, Western values are having a pervasive and accelerating influence on the world's industry, technology, law, politics, life-style, diet, language, alphabet, religion, and philosophy.

The ongoing process of globalization has accelerated this process. On top of largely Western government systems such as democracy and constitution, many Western technologies and customs like music, clothing and cars have been introduced across various parts of the world and copied and created in traditionally non-western countries like India, China, Japan etc.

The main characteristics here are economic liberalization (free trade) and democratization, combined with the spread of an individualized culture. After the breakup of the USSR in 1991, many of its component states and allies also underwent Westernization, including privatisation of hitherto state-controlled industry.

Western economic systems have produced some improvements in areas such as technology, transport and the provision of essential and nonessential goods and services. However, as industrial economies continue to grow in a finite world the overall impact is increasingly negative. Inefficient use of resources, high levels of pollution and numerous social disruptions resulting from industrialization have caused human society to be grossly unsustainable.

Studies by the World Resources Institute and many others show that, with some regional exceptions, every life support system on the planet is in decline (i.e.: clean air, clean water, forests, topsoil, aquifers, fisheries, wetlands, biodiversity, etc.). Social pressure and turmoil are increasing around the world, driven by a widening gap between rich and poor and other factors. Social distress is evident even in prosperous regions. Americans, for example, medicate themselves with food (two thirds are overweight, one third are obese), television (four hours per day on average), and antidepressants drugs (rapidly growing use).

"The Westerners will attempt to remake the native culture within their own image, ignoring the fact that the models of culture that they have created are inappropriate for settings outside of Western civilisation" —*Conrad Phillip Kottak*

3.

Western Economic Model

Based On Greed And Exploitation

Western economic model has its roots in colonization and it grew out of reckless exploitation of colonies' resources. The development of the West assumed limitless resources for the colonizers, since development of the colonies themselves was never an issue in a fragmented world where colonies were mere geographical spreads whose natural resources existed for the benefit of the European or English economies. In other words, the Industrial Revolution in the western economies and their consequent prosperity were possible thanks to severe underpricing of raw material sourced from their colonies, as well as underpricing of labour - through slave trade, as well as indentured and exploited labour

This legacy of exploitation continues till date, though under a different nomenclature. Multinational corporations are the new face of colonizers and migrant labour in Asia and South America are the modern slaves.

Modern capitalism has the distinct colonial streak in that it seeks to benefit and thrive at every turn by underpricing everything. In a constrained world, there is urgent necessity to reject the Western consumption-led growth model where everything can be traded and has a price, but is actually underpriced to suit the needs of vested interests, industry and its lobbyists.

Colonies do not cease to be colonies because they are independent. —Benjamin Disraeli

This is only possible if we evolve a nature and people friendly economic model and that there is a government with some scruples. Such a government has to stand up to vested interests and also the mainly Western-led international bodies which are wedded to the notion of the "globalization of everything and anything" through free markets, free trade, the power of technology and the leveraging of finance.

The western model of development that has its roots in 18th, 19th and 20th centuries is not suitable for developing countries like India or China in the 21st century.

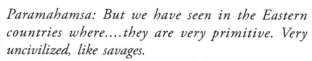

Paramahamsa: But we have seen in the Eastern countries where....they are very primitive. Very uncivilized, like savages.
Amogha: They don't have enough food.
Paramahamsa: No technology, no education.
Prabhupada: Because you have plundered them for the last so many centuries. You rascals, you have plundered. You have taken all their money, all their jewels, all their gold, and made British Museum. (laughter)
—Morning Walk, May 10, 1975, Perth

4.

Western Economic Model Has Lost Relevance

Does Not Belong To The 21st Century

The year 2011 saw the downgrading of America's credit rating. I was a significant event in the 250 year old history of industrial revolution. This is indicative of an era which would witness the demise of capitalism and industrialism.

Once the Western way was seen to deliver gleaming cities, efficient societies and powerful, self-confident countries. Now it appears to deliver sclerotic and crisis-prone economies, government dysfunction and social unrest.

The West no longer is the mirror in which the rest of the world sees the future it hopes for. And alongside the apparent ebbing of the West's significance and authority, there are real questions about its future as an entity. Once not so long ago the West was defined clearly both by what it stood for, and what it stood against.

Modern capitalism is now a model of an entrenched political and economic ideology and at the same time has historical underpinnings based on colonialism and therefore global privilege with access to unlimited resources (example: colonies such as India, African nations or frontier land such as Australia). As such it  does not belong in the 21st century where all the scientific evidence points to limits being surpassed on numerous fronts as the resource crunch sets in. This model does not believe that there are limits and that we live in a finite world.

5.

Inherently Instable Systems

Modern economic system is artificial and it is against the natural and harmonious way of living in this material world. It is hardly two hundred years old and being kept in place by great manipulative endeavors. The system keeps slipping and the governments and industry keep propping it up. But something as artificial as this can not be continued forever. Curtains have to come down on every dramatic performance, however interesting or great the show may be.

History of Western economic system is a history of crashes. One such great crash was not so long ago. On 21st January 2008, known as Black Monday, investors in India lost Rs 6 trillion within minutes of the Indian Stock Exchange's opening in Mumbai. The authorities immediately suspended the trading for one hour. The sensex tumbled 2,029 points within minutes of start of trading.

Small investors were advised to stay away from the markets. Investors' wealth - measured in terms of cumulative market capitalisation of all the listed companies - declined by a whopping Rs 18,40,173 crore.

As per information available on the Bombay Stock Exchange website, the total market capitalisation stood at Rs 59,53,525 crore at the end of the Black Monday's trading against Rs 71,38,810 crore before the stock exchange began business on that day.

The cause for this was attributed on concerns regarding the US economy going into recession. Apart from the story of January 2008 in India, by October 2008, investors across the world lost more than $10 trillion - an amount more than 10 times of the entire investor wealth in India.

All 52 equity markets of the world suffered a loss of $10.5 trillion in 2008 as per the leading rating agency and financial data provider, Standard and Poors. Indian stock market valuation nearly halved in 2008.

It was all a classic repeat of year 1929. In 1929, America was having an economic explosion. Immigrants were pouring in. There were more jobs than people. Farmers were leaving their fields for factories, making twice the income for half the labor. Politicians confidently portrayed a picture of an endless era of unprecedented prosperity. The prophets of gloom and doom were ignored as being fanatical crazies.

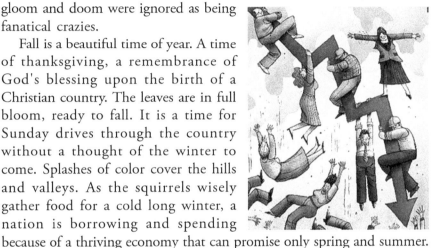

Fall is a beautiful time of year. A time of thanksgiving, a remembrance of God's blessing upon the birth of a Christian country. The leaves are in full bloom, ready to fall. It is a time for Sunday drives through the country without a thought of the winter to come. Splashes of color cover the hills and valleys. As the squirrels wisely gather food for a cold long winter, a nation is borrowing and spending because of a thriving economy that can promise only spring and summer.

A ship sails to England in the early part of October, full of wealthy entrepreneurs, a sign of absolute faith in a thriving American economy. While they were on their carefree vacation, enjoying the pleasure away from the stress of their jobs, a powerful economic tremor rippled through the United States. On October 24, 1929, 12,000,000 shares of common stocks traded in a single afternoon. By Monday, October 28th, the trading averages had dropped by 20 points. On Tuesday, October 29th, virtually all trades were to sell. It became 'A Nightmare On Wall Street.' Investors became panic–stricken, resulting in a huge economic land slide. Sixteen million shares were traded at a loss of 10 billion dollars. This was equivalent to twice the amount of currency of the entire USA. Headlines proclaimed, Wall Street Crashes. Tens of millions of people's life savings became completely useless. Millionaires were reduced to the unemployed. On Wall Street, it rained the bodies of men jumping from their offices high above. When the ship returned full of happy–go–lucky entrepreneurs, they were worth the clothes on their backs. An economic winter had fallen upon America which would effect the entire earth. An ice age that would last a decade.

The world has always hoped against the hope..until the reality stares in its face. There are important lessons to be learnt from the history but more often than not, we fail to do so.

There are limits to growth and the world economy has crossed those limits. In last 5 decades, world economy has been globalized and its not the best thing to have happened to our finances. The economic system built on a need for constant growth obviously can't last long in a finite world. Small is beautiful...and sustainable.

John Maynard Keynes said in 1927. "We will not have any crashes in our time." Dr Irving Fisher, another distinguished economist, said on October 17, 1929. "Stock prices have reached what looks like a permanently high plateau." US Treasury Secretary and Harvard Economic Society, among others, publicly shared their confidence.

They were reflecting on the state of the economy that was booming. It was a time when drivers and window cleaners eves-dropped on the conversations of their patrons to collect tips on shares. The DJ Index doubled from little less than 200 when Keynes made his prediction to almost 400 when Dr Fisher announced the high plateau of the state of the market. Within two weeks of Dr Fisher's forecast, it had crashed by over 40% to reach 200 again. By 1933, the DJ Index lost 90% of its value from the day of Dr Fisher's 'high plateau' proclamation to reach 40. Industrial production declined by two-thirds. The prices of farm land collapsed to nothing. The United States imposed high trade barriers, inviting retaliation by 25 other countries. Since Europe was dependent on exports to pay its World War I debts and Japan to be able to import the most basic necessities of life, high trade barriers devastated their economies. The Germans elected Hitler, a failed artist, to lead them. In Japan, too, nationalist extremism grew at a fast pace. The World War II followed from 1939 to 1945. History shows that bad finances and wars are the twins.

October: This is one of the peculiarly dangerous months to speculate in stocks. The others are July, January, September, April, November, May, March, June, December, August and February. —Mark Twain

The recent developments in the USA and Western Europe show that the existing economic model, which depends on continuous growth in production and consumption of material goods, is inherently unstable. Despite injection of massive public money the USA and West European countries continue to be bogged down with severe unemployment which is running to more than 10 per cent of the workforce. The massive public debt of Greece and other southern European nations such as Spain, Portugal and Italy has threatened the stability of the European economy. To save the economy of Greece, the EU has given it a massive bailout package, but this has put a question mark on the future of the Euro itself. The European Union countries are threatened with double dip recession whose contagion effect may spread to the global economy.

The Western economic model is built on debt and short term cycles. Therefore it snaps every few years into a recession. In 2011 economists are trying to figure out how they can prevent the next collapse. When the U.S. financial system was prevented from collapsing in 1997 (the Long Term Capital Management collapse), we got the tech market collapse of 2000-02. When the Fed did everything to mitigate the collapse of the tech market, they got the housing bust of 2007-09. When the housing bust turned into the global financial crisis, the government did everything it could to mitigate the collapse. Now many are wondering if we will experience a double-dip recession in 2011-12.

The global economic crisis, which started in 2008 with the USA as its epi-centre and whose contagion effect has spread all over the world, including India, has led policy-makers to abandon the philosophy of free and unbridled markets. In order to revive the economy, the USA,

> *"The United States have developed a new weapon that destroys people but it leaves buildings standing. It's called the stock market."*
> —*Jay Leno*

Britain and other developed countries have poured trillions of dollars of public money into the economy and have reverted to Keynesianism as an economic ideology. The state's direct intervention in the economy is in direct opposition to the ruling economic philosophy of the last three decades, which was characterised by an ideology of free markets, deregulation, liberalisation, privatisation and globalisation with the state exercising minimal interference in economic activities.

The current global economic meltdown has exposed the hollowness of the philosophy of unfettered capitalism with its belief in free and unregulated markets. Economic instability is built into the capitalist market economic system. Economic meltdown is inherent in the capitalist economy.

"The day the stock market crashed I was standing on a corner with a cop. I was a kid, a Wall Street runner. All of a sudden people started jumping out windows. I said, 'Murphy, you gotta do something He said, 'There ain't nothin' I can do.' What a mess! But my father, he didn't jump out a no window. He said, 'The good Lord will take care of us. And He did."
—*Dante Molinari*

6.
Debt Based Global Economy

Sinking In A Pit of Debts

The global economy is really a "debt-based" economy in that the economic development is fueled by issuing more and more debt. As soon as the flow of debt stops, economic development stops. Every country in the world follows this debt-based growth model.

The worldwide average of debt-to-GDP ratio stands at a whopping 90.8%. In an analysis of the world's 75 largest economies, Western-European and North American countries dominate the upper end of the spectrum, with Switzerland (422%) and the United Kingdom (408%) at the number two and three spots, respectively, and Ireland representing the most drastic debt-to-GDP ratio. According to the most recent World Bank data, Ireland's number stands at a staggering 1,267%. The 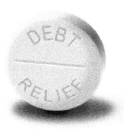 United States has the 20th largest debt-to-GDP ratio, standing at 98%.

In a debt-based economy, money is entirely created from debt. If all debt was retired in the country, there would be no money. Deflation is defined as a reduction in the credit/money supply. Everytime a loan is created it increases the money supply. Once that loan is retired, the money that was created is also retired.

This would all be different if the money was actually printed. But only a very small fraction of money created is actually ever printed. Only the money needed to carry our day to day transactions is printed. Near all of our money is nothing more than book entries, or today, a computer entry.

A fiat debt based money system requires inflation. If you go and buy a house on debt, at first you may have a hard time affording it. But due to inflation your wages increase and after a few years your mortgage payment becomes less and less of a percentage of your income. Same with the government. They borrow but they know that due to inflation their revenues will increase. So this huge debt, in theory, becomes less and less percentage of revenue.

Currently the subprime markets are seeing increasing defaults. When a debt is retired, it decreases the money supply. That computer entry that created the money is now zero. That money is gone into thin air from which it came. Debt can also be retired by default or a debt being forgiven. So massive defaults are deflationary, they take money out of the system.

In 1992 US public debt figure stood at $3 trillion and in 2000 it marginally rose to $3.4 trillion. During the presidency of George W. Bush, the gross public debt increased from $5.7 trillion in January 2001 to $10.7 trillion by December 2008. Under President Barack Obama, the debt increased from $10.7 trillion in 2008 to $14.73 trillion by September 2011. Situation has increasingly become difficult to manage and this has lead to credit downgrade of US treasuries.

In 1929, the debt ratio in relation to the America's Gross National Product stood at a healthy 16%. In 2011, the national debt has increased to an alarming 98% of the GNP. The total debt of America is greater than the combined external debts of all the nations of the world.

America's current debt as on September 2011 is $47,332 per American. The US national debt has continued to increase an average of $3.93 billion per day since September 2007.

Of course, in 2011, its the Euro debt crisis that the world is watching with bated breath. This is being described as being worse than 2008 crisis in US. The U.S. Treasury Department in 2008 helped devise and implement the myriad liquidity programs used to recapitalize big banks

Blessed are the young, for they will inherit the national debt. ~Herbert Hoover

and reassure investors when questions arose over their stability and integrity of deposits.

But uncertainty over what would happen in a run on European banks has added to the volatility of the European debt crisis and everyone is tossing around the words million, billion and trillion.

Have we become numb to the numbers?

Number' itself can be pronounced as 'number' or 'numb-er.' And maybe in this case, the latter is a better pronunciation. Until now such big numbers were never heard that often.

To provide some perspective on just how big a trillion dollars is, think about it like this: A trillion dollars is the number 1 followed by 12 zeroes. Or we can think of it this way: One trillion $1 bills stacked one on top of the other would reach nearly 68,000 miles (about 109,400 kilometers) into the sky, or about a third of the way from the Earth to the moon.

To put a trillion dollars in another context, if we spend a million dollars every day since Jesus was born, we still wouldn't have spent a trillion. A million dollars a day for 2,000 years is only three-quarters of a trillion dollars.

Back in 1993, President Bill Clinton wanted a $30 billion jobs and investment package. He didn't get it. Few years ago President Bush signed an emergency economic stimulus of $168 billion - a tally that seems paltry compared with the amounts requested today. But consider this: If all of the financial market interventions, loans, guarantees, bailouts and rescues are approved, they will total more than $7 trillion.

Third World Debt

In comparison, notable countries which have extremely low debt-to-GDP ratios are Brazil (13%), Singapore (10.7%), China (4.7%) and India (4.6%), with the lowest ratio boasted by Algeria, at 1.2%. Too low a ratio may not necessarily be a good thing either, and could reflect a combination of lacked foreign investment, low confidence in the nation's finances or the absence of debt-funded growth and investment policies by the national government.

The International Monetary Fund (IMF) was set up to provide an international reserve of money supposedly to help nations with big deficits. In practice it makes matters worse because a nation with a big deficit has to seek a bail out from the IMF. But this comes in the form of a loan, repayable with interest. Like loans from a commercial bank, IMF loans are money created out of nothing, based on a cash reserve pool, which is provided by western nations who go into debt to provide it.

The nation with the deficit keeps getting even more heavily into debt but it continues to be able to carry on trading and importing goods from the wealthier nations. As a result, much of this borrowed IMF loan money flows into the economies of wealthier Western nations. However, the repayment obligation, including the interest payments, remains with the debtor nation.

This is the horror of third world debt — the poorest nations borrow money to bolster the money supply of the richer nations. In order to secure income to pay the loan and interest, and redress the trade balance, these poorest nations must export whatever they can produce.

Thus they exploit every possible resource — stripping forests for timber, mining, giving over their best agricultural land to providing luxury foodstuffs for the West, rather than providing for local needs.

Today, for nations in Africa, Central and South America and elsewhere, the revenue from their exports does not even meet the interest payments on these IMF loans.

The sums paid in interest over the years far exceed the amounts of the original loans themselves. The result is a desperate shortage of money in their economies — resulting in cutbacks in necessities such as basic health and education programmes.

There are 10^11 stars in the galaxy. That used to be a huge number. But it's only a hundred billion. It's less than the national deficit! We used to call them astronomical numbers. Now we should call them economical numbers.
-Richard Feynman (1918 - 1988)

Grinding poverty exists in nations with a great wealth of natural resources. Structural Adjustment Programmes are now attached to IMF loans and include conditions that recipient countries will reduce or remove tariff barriers and "open up their markets to foreign competition" - in other words take surplus goods off to another country that can't be sold at home.

War

War means enormous increases in national debt and enormous profits for the banks. Massive government borrowing and money creation by banks is required to fund a war effort. Financiers and bankers have covertly funded both sides in both World Wars and many other conflicts before and since.

Having profited from war, leaving nations with massive debts and more beholden than ever to them, the banks then fund reconstruction.

One thing is clear: if we have learned anything from the global economic crisis, the policy of taking on excessive debt cannot be perpetually sustained, no matter the size of a debtor nation's domestic economy. Chanakya, an ancient Indian philosopher, may have one piece of advice for these nations, "Three things should be taken care of immediately: fire, disease and debt. Otherwise they spiral out of control in no time."

7.

Bank Runs And Currency Collapse

Prior to the 1800s, savers looking to keep their valuables in safekeeping depositories deposited gold coins and silver coins at goldsmiths, receiving in turn a note for their deposit. Once these notes became a trusted medium of exchange an early form of paper money was born, in the form of the goldsmiths' notes.

As the notes were used directly in trade, the goldsmiths observed that people would not usually redeem all their notes at the same time, and saw the opportunity to invest coin reserves in interest-bearing loans and bills. This left the goldsmiths with more notes on issue than reserves to pay them with. This generated income—a process that altered their role from passive guardians of bullion charging fees for safe storage, to interest-paying and earning banks. Thus 'Fractional-reserve banking' was born.

However, if creditors (note holders of gold originally deposited) lost faith in the ability of a bank to redeem (pay) their notes, many would try to redeem their notes at the same time. If in response a bank could not raise enough funds by calling in loans or selling bills, it either went into insolvency or defaulted on its notes. Such a situation is called a bank run and has caused the demise of many banks.

On 30th September 2008, Wall Street's worries made their way to India as ICICI Bank, the country's largest private-sector bank, saw thousands of clients withdrawing cash at its branches and ATMs on rumors that the bank could fail. India's central bank, The Reserve Bank of India, in an unprecedented move, issued a statement saying there was enough liquidity at ICICI Bank and it arranged to provide adequate cash to the bank to meet the demands of customers.

The collapse of Washington Mutual bank around the same time in 2008, the largest bank failure in history, is an example of a "silent run" on the bank, where depositors removed vast sums of money from the bank through electronic transfer.

In 2009, the number of shuttered banks in US alone was 140 and in 2010 it grew to 157. A report released by the Federal Deposit Insurance Corporation (FDIC) said more banks are expected to fail in 2011. The figure is the worst since 1992 when a savings-and-loan crisis hit the country. More alarming is that the FDIC has a list of 860 problem banks.

Because of the spate of bank failures, the FDIC coffers are depleted, although the agency forecast it will have sufficient funds in the future to address an expected rise in bank closures until 2014.

This is just a news from US, the world's financial giant. Elsewhere the situation is equally bad. When the banks go down, can the currencies be far behind?

In year 2008, many currencies followed the path of these banks. Iceland, Argentina, Hungary, Ukraine and others all saw a sharp fall in the value of their currencies.

When a currency loses the confidence of its people, its fall becomes exponential, as has happened to the Zimbabwe dollar. In 1982 one US dollar equalled one Zimbabwe dollar. Today around Z$200,000 buys one US $1. During World War II, German mark was used for making cigars. Rampant inflation, Current account deficits, lower interest rates, these all contribute to the currency collapse. Most of the currencies in the world, including major ones, have no asset backing. Governments simply print money whenever they need it or a crisis hits them. This

"Inflation is when you pay fifteen dollars for the ten-dollar haircut you used to get for five dollars when you had hair." - Sam Ewing

leads to inflation and when a currency gets completely discredited, it collapses. Today the US dollar, the world currency, is in real danger of collapsing. US Treasuries have been stripped of their AAA rating, which may be the beginning of a process that leads to the loss of the dollar's vital status as the world's reserve currency.

World experts in money markets like Warren Buffet and George Soros are betting on a major crash of the dollar in the near future. They think it will be greater than the Great Depression of the 1930s. With trade deficits of over 650 billion last year America is placing its future in the hands of non-Americans. It is now, roughly 6.5 percent of the total economy. Their deficit is financed by the central banks of countries like China and Japan. In fact all the world banks are chock-full of US dollars, much more than they want or need for trade.

If the dollar collapses the whole world economy collapses because there is no alternative yet to the dollar. Right now if the dollar crashes so would the economies of China, Japan, India and dozens of other countries and much of their holdings are in American banks.

Right now, the US dollar is probably 40 per cent overvalued versus the Japanese yen or the Chinese Yuan. The fear in the short term is that some one may dump the dollar and start a dollar run. Just like the stock market, the first out is going to loose the least money and everyone else will be holding dollars at less value. What if some small Islamic country decides they have too many dollars and dumps $10 billion all at once? Panic will set in the rest of the world, and everyone will start getting out of the dollar leaving those holding dollars with half its present value.

What is saving the dollar is not faith in the dollar but the lack of an alternative. In 2011, euro has occupied the main stage in terms of fragility and the world attention and concern have shifted from dollar to euro.

> "Bank failures are caused by depositors who don't deposit enough money to cover losses incurred by the management"
> ~Dan Quayle (American 44th US Vice President)

8.

The Day An Economic Holocaust Was Averted

Economies Can Collapse At The Speed of Light

The Story of First Electronic Bank Run

Rep. Paul Kanjorski, a US Congressman reveals an incident: "On Thursday [the 18th Sept. 2008], at about 11 o'clock in the morning, the Federal Reserve noticed a tremendous drawdown of money market accounts in the United States to a tune of $550 billion being drawn out in a matter of an hour or two. The Treasury opened up its window to help. They pumped $105 billion into the system and quickly realized that they could not stem the tide. We were having an electronic run on the banks. They decided to close the operation, close down the money accounts, and announce a guarantee of $250,000 per account so there wouldn't be further panic and there. And that's what actually happened. If they had not done that their estimation was that by two o'clock that afternoon, $5.5 trillion would have been drawn out of the money market system of the United States, would have collapsed the entire economy of the United States, and within 24 hours the world economy would have collapsed. Now we talked at that time about what would have happened if that happened. It would have been the end of our economic system and our political system as we know it."

He further adds, "We [in Congress] talked at that time about what would have happened. It would've been the end of our economic system and our political system as we know it. That's why, when they made the point that we had to act quickly, we did. Secretary Paulson said let's buy out the sub-prime mortgages, but he said give us latitude and large authority to do as many things as we decide necessary and give us $700 billion to do that."

He continues, "Shortly after we [American Congress] enacted our bill with those very broad powers, the UK [English Parliament] came out and said, No, we [the UK] don't have enough money to buy all the toxic assets; instead we're going to put our money into banks so their equity grows and they're not bankrupt.

"The UK started that process. And it was true that it was much cheaper to put more money into banks as equity investments than to start buying their bad assets which would cost $3 or $4 trillion of taxpayers' money to buy these bad assets and we didn't have that kind of money. We only had $700 billion."

Finally He adds, "So Paulson went in and made a complete switch and started buying securities and reinvesting in banks of the United States. Why? Because if you don't have a banking system, you don't have an economy. And although we did that, it wasn't enough money and as fast as we did that the economy has been falling. And the reason last week is that we are no better off today than we were three months ago

"Fill the bag up?.. With what?!"

because we've had a decrease in other equity positions of the banks because other assets are going sour by the moment."

This narrative by Rep. Paul Kanjorski is a case of electronic bank run and its giving nightmares to the world's banking system. People don't have to stand in line outside the banks and create a scene. People can withdraw their investments from the privacy of their own homes by means of the internet. That means "instantaneous" bank runs can take place at almost the speed of light anytime the public panics.

All by itself, that's a scary thought. In this first electronic bank run, $550 billion was withdrawn in "an hour or two". But this was a bank run/panic that happened so quickly and "stealthily" that almost no one knew about it at the time—including the participants. Thus, it's possible

"What is the crime of robbing a bank compared with the crime of founding one." ~ *Earl Warren*

that less than 1% of the American people unwittingly participated in this $550 bank run.

What caused this electronic bank run? Was it a conspiracy among some elite group? No. It was the spontaneous, uncoordinated actions of thousands, perhaps a few million Americans who reacted to some news event (perhaps the closing of another bank) independently but simultaneously deciding to withdraw their money from their 'money accounts' and move it somewhere else.

Thus, there was a kind of 'panic'—but no one who participated in the panic realized a 'panic' was taking place. In other words, on September 18th, I might've read the news about another bank failure and decided on my own that it would be prudent to use my internet connection to move some of my bank funds. I might thereby have participated in this first electronic bank run, but I would not have dreamt that hundreds of thousands of others were also reacting to the same news event (perhaps a bank failure) and simultaneously also withdrawing their funds from the banks.

Fortunately, virtually no one but the Federal Reserve and the Treasury Department recognized that an electronic bank run was taking place. If the rest of America had realized a 'national' bank run was taking place, the whole country would've joined in and every dime might've been pulled out of the banks in a matter of minutes.

Probably what saved the day was the fact that this electronic bank run occurred 'privately' and without the knowledge of the public or even the participants. Therefore, although there was a true 'bank run,' there was no 'panic' in the public in a real psychological sense.

Even so, this 'spontaneous' electronic bank run had to terrify the people in Congress, at the Treasury Department and in the Federal Reserve. Thanks to digital dollars and internet connections to bank accounts, the people can now randomly, spontaneously and unpredictably decide to withdraw so much money from their bank accounts, that the whole U.S. and global economies could instantly collapse.

In other words, on this day, the 'masters of the universe' in Washington D.C. learned they are no longer in control of the monetary system and economy. Thanks to digital dollars and the internet, 'money' can now move at the speed of light and virtually anyone (everyone) can move his (their) money at any time for any rhyme, reason or whim. If enough people decide to move their cash based on single news report, the whole banking system and global economies can be collapsed at the speed of light.

Revelation 18:14-18—which describes the "end times" fall of "Babylon" and reads in part: "For in one hour such great riches came to nothing." When—in all the previous history of the world—could all the "riches" of a mighty nation "come to nothing" in just "one hour"? Such fantastic destruction of "wealth" could not have been possible until 1) we started treating debt  instruments (promises to pay) as if they were assets (payments); 2) we devised digital "dollars" that consisted of nothing more than electronic 1's and 0's on some banker's hard drive; and 3) the internet allowed masses of people to access their bank accounts almost instantly.

For virtually 5,000 years of human history, the event described in Revelation 18:14-18 was not merely impossible, it was unimaginable. It was inconceivable. How could you make all the wealth (gold and silver coin) of a nation "come to nothing" in just "one hour"? Sure, the gold and silver might be stolen, or even sunk to the bottom of the sea, but it would continue to exist and would not "come to nothing".

Today, however, digital dollars can "come to nothing"—and they can do so at the speed of light. In fact, these bank runs prove that Revelation 18:14-18 is no longer impossible, but is now even likely.

Think not? How many people are currently plugged into electronic banking? Given the global awareness of the current economic crisis, let's suppose the stock market fell by 1,000 points in one day, war broke out in the Middle East, or martial law was suddenly imposed in a big country—could any one of those or scores of similar events be enough to trigger a massive, spontaneous withdrawal of bank funds over the internet? Yes. And we only need one such event to collapse the global economy.

According to Congressman Kanjorski, this electronic bank run came within a few hours of collapsing the whole world economy. If this first

It's morally wrong to allow a sucker to keep his money. ~ WC Fields

electronic bank run had continued for just a few more hours, the entire global economy would have collapsed.

So what happens if there's a second electronic bank run, the public gets wind of it, and just 10% of the people start pulling money out of their bank accounts? This particular electronic bank run was probably caused by just a few hundred thousand depositors. What happens if just ten million depositors participate in the next electronic bank run? The global economy dies—and it dies that day.

Can we see the insanity of storing our wealth in a digital (or paper) form? The whole global, paper-money/digital-money economy can completely shatter in as little as a few hours.

Today we don't need any rockets or atomic weapons to destroy the world. All you need is the internet and a bunch of panicked bank depositors. An electronic World War III could be launched any time by some small percentage of people panicking simultaneously and pulling their money out of bank accounts over the internet. There is no single "red button" in the control of the US President or Russian Premier. Control is now 'democratically' dispersed to everyone with an internet connection and electronic access to bank accounts. Virtually all of us have an electronic trigger that—when pushed simultaneously with that of a few million others—could precipitate an electronic catastrophe.

What's the fundamental strength of a banking system built on paper promises to pay that can't be kept, 'assets' that are really debt instruments and digital (illusory) dollars?

Today, we don't have any 'money' in its true sense. All we have are paper pounds and electronic digits which may be 'currency,' but these are not 'money'.

That's why we're in an unprecedented economic mess of biblical proportions. The problem is not one of numbers or magnitude. It's not about the interest rate or the unemployment rate. It's not about 800

When a person with money meets a person with experience, the person with the experience winds up with the money and the person with the money winds up with the experience. ~ *Harvey MacKay*

billion versus 2 trillion. It's about the substance of the things being measured. 800 billion what? 2 trillion what? Digital "dollars"? Digital dollars don't really exist. Digital dollars are illusions on a hard drive. I could store $1 quadrillion on a $100 hard drive. And yet, even if I stored $1 quadrillion on my hard drive, would my $100 hard drive be worth $1 quadrillion—or just $100?

That's the crux of the problem. The whole system is based on illusions. It's based on lies called paper and digital 'dollars' rather than the gold and silver.

But illusion only work so long as the people don't really see it. As people begin to see the illusion, the illusion and its power necessarily disappears. Its high time to realize that a 'derivative' that reads "$100,000" is not really one hundred thousand actual dollars, but only a fancy piece of paper. As a result, billions and even trillions of illusory, imaginary derivatives, bonds and stocks are literally disappearing and thereby causing the collapse of the banking system that's built on illusions. And the system's only remedy is to issue more illusions!

The current economic 'problems' started with public recognition that a substantial number of mortgages (paper promises to pay) were 'non-performing assets' (worthless). Then the system began to downgrade a number of bonds as 'under-performing assets' (semi-worthless).

All of these non-performing and under-performing debt instruments have been categorized as 'toxic assets' (worthless). How does the system plan to deal with these 'toxic assets'? By buying them with legal tender (Federal Reserve Notes, paper currency and digital dollars).

What fundamental difference exists between these various forms of 'legal tender' and the current 'toxic assets'? How are these paper and digital dollars fundamentally different from paper bonds or paper stocks or paper derivatives? The truth is that there's no fundamental difference between these paper/digital dollars (legal tender) and 'toxic assets'. Although the world has not quite yet recognized that truth, our paper/digital dollars are, themselves, 'toxic assets'.

I finally know what distinguishes man from other beasts: financial worries. — *Jules Renard*

And the governments are trying to diffuse a crisis caused by 'toxic assets' by purchasing them with something even more toxic.

We have to realize that the problem is systemic and can not be cured within the existing system or by the existing system. The 'system' itself—the one that issues and relies on illusions—is the problem.

(With Thanks to Alfred Adask for his contribution)

When a man spends his own money to buy something for himself, he is very careful about how much he spends and how he spends it. When a man spends his own money to buy something for someone else, he is still very careful about how much he spends, but somewhat less what he spends it on. When a man spends someone else's money to buy something for himself, he is very careful about what he buys, but doesn't care at all how much he spends. And when a man spends someone else's money on someone else, he doesn't care how much he spends or what he spends it on. And that's government for you.
~Milton Friedman

9.

Paper Currency And Inflation
A World of Cheaters And Cheated

Following is a morning walk conversation between His Divine Grace A.C.Bhaktivedanta Swami Prabhupada and some of his students, recorded on December 31, 1973 in Los Angeles.

Prajapati: Actually, I was concerned this morning about inflation. The government and the newspapers, they say the biggest problem today is inflation. From our Krsna conscious standpoint, how can we cure this problem of inflation?

Prabhupada: It is very simple. Don't accept paper currency. It must be gold or some metal worth. Just like one dollar, it must be worth one dollar metal. Then it is solved. But they want to cheat. How it can be solved? Because if I pay you one dollar, I must pay you value for one dollar. But it is the cheating process is going on, "I pay you one dollar, a piece of paper. That's all." So you accept cheating, and I also cheat. Government allows. So how the problem can be solved?

When you or I write a check there must be sufficient funds in our account to cover that check, but when the Federal Reserve writes a check, it is creating money.
— Boston Federal Reserve Bank

Prajapati: In the economy itself there isn't actually enough money to, that's even in the banks...

Prabhupada: Therefore I say cheating. I have no money. I give you simply paper. I promise to pay hundred dollars. What is the use of that promise if I have no money? But you want to be cheated. I cheat you. That's all.

Bahulasva: Real money is gold and silver.

Prabhupada: Any... It must be valuable. Whatever it may be. Gold is taken, because gold is the most valuable metal. A small piece of gold, it can carry two hundred dollars. But if I give you iron, then you have to bring another, what is called, bus, to carry it. (laughter) So therefore gold standard is accepted everywhere. There is a standard price of gold, so when I pay you money, it must carry the value in gold. That's all. Then there is no inflation. The people want to be cheated, and people cheat. That's all.

So a worker is getting three thousand dollar per month, but he is getting paper. But he is thinking that "I am getting money." He is giving his labor, and things are being produced. This is the policy. "Cheat him. Without giving money, give him paper, and get his labor, and produce goods." This is modern economy. Is it not? A laborer, a worker, is given high salary, high wages. So what he is getting? It is paper. And he is very enthusiastic to give his labor. So production is more. And when you go to purchase the products, then you have to pay again. Whatever you have earned, you have to pay everything, pay to the bank or pay to the man. Simply cheating process is going on...

Everyone can understand this is pure cheating. I give you a hundred dollars, a piece of paper. That's all. And you accept it. You want to be cheated. You thought, that "I have got now daily, hundred dollars. So let me work very hard." He does not consider that "I am not getting a hundred dollars. I am getting a piece of paper." So people have no brain

The modern Banking system manufactures money out of nothing. The process is perhaps the most astounding piece of sleight of hand that was ever invented. Banks can in fact inflate, mint and unmint the modern ledger-entry currency.
~L. L. B. Angus

to understand even. "This is not hundred dollars. Give me cash, hundred dollars."

Then there will be no inflation. Because I know that paying you a piece of paper, I can cheat you, therefore I am printing notes, to cheat so many people. Therefore inflation. But when there will be no possibility to cheat you, then there will be no inflation. Here I have got the opportunity, because I know that pushing forward a piece of paper, I can cheat so many people. So there must be inflation. Is it not? This is not psychological? If I know that I can cheat you by this instrument, so why shall I not increase that? That is inflation.

Karandhara: The governments actually started the whole thing. They instituted paper money and they instituted it because it is a cheating process. But everyone is participating. So it is just going on and on. That is the real cause of inflation.

Prabhupada: Yes. That's it. They are getting encouragement in their cheating business.

Bahulasva: They won't let you have any gold.

Prabhupada: Now they have made law that you cannot store gold?

Karandhara: That's been since 1933.

Prabhupada: Just see.

Karandhara: Americans cannot own gold, store gold. Pretty soon they are going to pass the same law for silver. Now they have introduced a law that even the penny, which is the smallest denomination, it used to made out of copper, so now they are going to make it out of aluminum, because copper is too expensive.

Prabhupada: Just see.

Bahulasva: It will be worth less than a penny when it is made out of aluminum.

Prabhupada: Why not cement? (laughter) Because by law everything will be acceptable. Make it cement.

Prajapati: It seems all right for ordinary dealings, Srila Prabhupada,

"The business pages of American newspapers should not read like a scandal sheet."
George W. Bush (1946–), US former president
Referring to a series of high-profile accounting scandals.
Source: Speech (July 2002)

having this money, what's going on, but for large scale transactions it might be very difficult. And as the practical basis, transactions of thousands and thousands of dollars, would be...

Prabhupada: That will be good for the people. Because large scale transaction is there, therefore the capitalists are hoarding. Goods are there, everything is there. You pay black price, you get it. Then, when somebody's hoarding, he is not giving to the market. So if the large scale industry and trade becomes stopped, that is good for people.

HOW TO TURN THE ECONOMY AROUND		
Step 1	Step 2	Step 3

Suppose if you want to store, say, thousand kilos or a thousand bags of rice, so you have to pay me gold. But you have no such gold. Therefore large scale industry will be stopped. Just see.

Karandhara: Then the price of rice would go very low.

Prabhupada: Yes. Then you get actual price and actual value. Goods are there, any part of the world you..., there is enough commodity. But these rascals, they are hoarding, and they are not giving in right time. So people are suffering.

Karandhara: Yes. There's a... They buy now. They buy the goods before they are even grown, from the commodity market.

Prabhupada: Yes, because they can pay in this paper, the bank will advance. So as soon as you... You have to introduce this metal coins, value. The whole cheating scheme will fail.

Karandhara: Whenever there is an economic depression, then gold remains valuable. Just like when the stock market crashed in 1929, if you had gold you could still purchase goods. No matter how bad the economy was, people would accept gold as barter, but not currency.

Prabhupada: Yes. Indian economy was that if you have got extra

"All one great big lie."
Bernard Madoff, US former fund manager and former governor of NASDAQ, Confessing that his $50 billion investment fund was a total fraud.
Source: Quoted in the Independent (London) (December 16, 2008)

money, you get gold ornament for your wife. So then your money is stocked there. Or purchase some utensils, silver utensils. That was Indian economy. This depositing in the bank and thinking that I am getting good interest, that is another cheating. It is another cheating. If things are not available, what will you get by getting interest? Therefore I am advising that purchase land and produce our own food. There will be no problem.

Karandhara: The inflation rate is higher than the interest rate. If you earn 5 3/4 % interest in a year, the inflation has gone up 6% in a year. So actually your money, at best it's kept the same.

Prabhupada: The money is to be kept in cattle and grains. That is Indian economy, cattle and grains. If you have got many cows, you get milk. Milk preparations. And if you have got grain, then where is your problem? You prepare your foodstuff at home and eat and chant Hare Krsna. Where is your problem? You want to eat and live peacefully. So if you have got grains and milk, you have got enough food and there is no problem. You haven't got to go fifty miles for your work, and then you require a tin car. So many problems. But if you get your food at home, then eat them and chant Hare Krsna. Simple thing.

"Surely I'm not the only person to ask the obvious question: How different, really, is Mr. Madoff's tale from the story of the investment industry as a whole?"
Paul R. Krugman, US economist
On the fraudulent investment fund run by Bernie Madoff.
Source: New York Times (December 19, 2008)

10.
Remedies Worse Than The Disease

A system will reach a pre-collapse state before a collapse actually occurs. However, once it reaches a pre-collapse state the damage has already been done even though no collapse has actually occurred. Trying to suppress a collapse from a pre-collapse state will make the system unstable and prone to larger collapses in the future.

Current government policies all over the world are to seek economic stability through the suppression of collapses. Japan's lost decade(s) is an example of an economic crash that has been heavily mitigated. China may be in an even worse situation. It needs to consistently produce a yearly economic growth rate  of 8 percent or more in order to maintain a stable society. This requirement pretty much puts China on the expressway to a supercritical crash. We may see this sooner rather than later because China's real estate markets are overheated and may come crashing down in the next year or two.

The main reason we are heading towards Great Depression II is the obsession with recession avoidance by any means necessary, that we can have ever-lasting good times.

The recessions are necessary part of getting rid of bad investments and speculative games of boom times. If societies try to avoid them the end result is going to be eventually Long or even Great Depression.

Steve Forbes, CEO of Forbes Inc, feels that bad government policies are to blame for the economic woes all over the world. He feels that

poor government policymaking is the real
cause of our troubles and free markets work
better than government-dominated systems.
But we haven't had truly free markets in
recent times.

All of the economic disasters during the
last century have their origins in such
mischievous policies. For example Smoot-
Hawley Tariff triggered the Great Depression
and the Federal Reserve's binge of printing too much money, which
brought the Great Inflation of the 1970s and the Great Recession today.

Of course, its not just the government policies, but the system itself
is flawed. But the flawed government policies help bring out the worst
in the system and add icing on the cake.

An example of the frivolity of political class:

*"Markets caused the drama. Now they have to make sure to get
things straight again." -Angela Merkel, German Chancellor on
European financial crisis.*

*(This remark reveals in the German Chancellor a basic inability
even to grasp the nature, let alone understand the scale, of the
disaster facing Europe. Such a failure of comprehension is entirely
typical of leaders throughout history, at times of grave international
urgency.)*

11.

Emergence of Non-Western Actors

A New Financial World Order In Making

For the first time in at least 300 years, stage is being set for non-Western actors to play a major and dominant role in the world affairs. This is the major power shift of the last few centuries. Last year, the British political philosopher John Gray said that "the era of American global leadership is over... in a change as far-reaching in its implications as the fall of the Soviet Union, an entire model of government and the economy has collapsed".

The meltdown of some of the Wall Street's largest financial institutions in September 2008 underlined the shift in economic power from the West, with some of the fallen giants seeking support from sovereign wealth funds and the US government stepping in to save the mortgage titans. This was partly in order to reassure countries like China, which has invested huge sums of money in them: if they had withdrawn these, it would almost certainly have precipitated a collapse in the value of the dollar.

The financial crisis has graphically illustrated the disparity between an East Asia cash rich from decades of surpluses and a US cash-poor following many years of deficits.

These events point towards the fact that the American and European era is coming to an end, as the Western-oriented world order is replaced by one increasingly dominated by the East. The historian Niall Ferguson has written that the bloody twentieth century witnessed "the descent of the West" and "a reorientation of the world" toward the East. Realists go on to note that as China gets more powerful and the United States' position erodes, two things are likely to happen: China will try to use its growing influence to reshape the rules and institutions of the international system to better serve its interests, and other states in the system will start to see China as a growing security threat. The result of these developments, they predict, will be tension, distrust, and conflict, the typical features of a power transition. In this view, the drama of

Prabhupāda began to explain why for centuries "the sun did not set over the British Empire." Just as the modes of goodness, passion, and ignorance affect an individual, they also affect entire nations. In previous ages the mode of goodness predominated, and thus Vedic culture was spread throughout the world. But in Kali-yuga the modes of passion and ignorance are especially strong, and whichever nation wields the greatest physical strength is able to subjugate others. Although the Vedic civilization was unequaled, the British had been able to rule India for centuries on account of their predominance in the mode of passion. However, England's supremacy in world affairs had in the course of time diminished, until her glory had all but faded.

To make his point clear, Prabhupāda pointed with his cane to a large building still under construction. "Just see! The house is not yet completed, but someone is already living there. This means poverty. Britain is now finished. When they have to start renting the bottom floors before they finish the top, that means they have run out of money. They need to collect more money to pay for the upper stories to be completed." He further said in another conversation, "In England aristocracy is finished. They're all selling their property. They cannot maintain. Even the Queen cannot maintain her establishment, but because it's government.... The Buckingham Palace was not repaired for many years. Last time, when I went there, I saw it is repaired now. Before that, three, four times I went. It was blackish. The stone had become black. That means many years it was not repaired. There are aristocrat type statues now rolling on the ground. Who cares?

Prabhupāda's simple but brilliant example demonstrated how the changing influences of the modes of nature sway the course of world history, with even the greatest nations unable to avoid their kar (From 'Servant of The Servant')

China's rise will feature an increasingly powerful China and a declining United States locked in an epic battle over the rules and leadership of the international system. And as the world's largest country emerges not from within but outside the established post-World War II international order, it is a drama that will end with the grand ascendance of China and the onset of an Asian-centered world order.

So the 'third world' is trying to move up the slots as there are appearing signs of few openings up there. But will the 'third world' learn from the mistakes of the 'first world' or do the same things that made the 'first world' go down. There is a saying that if you keep doing the same thing, you'll keep getting the same result and Einstein defines insanity as doing the same thing over and over again and expecting different results. So now its upto the 'third world' to learn its lessons....from the mistakes of the 'first world'.

"Several times my typewriter and tape recorders were stolen and the police could not take any action. There are many persons in the Bowery Street; they have no shelter to live. So if a certain fraction of the people are supposed to be very materially happy at the cost of others, that is not material advancement. Had it been so, then why there are so many persons confused and frustrated? So actually there is no material advancement here. So the Western type of civilization, industrialism and capitalism, is no material advancement. It is material exploitation."
— *Srila Prabhupada (Letter, 14 March 1969)*

12.

Western Economic Model

Not Suitable For Underdeveloped Nations

Through centuries of conquest, colonialism and western 'development', the world has come to follow in the footsteps of the Western world, and copy their values, culture, lifestyle, diet and economics.

But there is a saying, 'One man's food is another's poison.' Every place on the Earth is unique. Each has its own particular soils, the product of eons of geological and biological activity, and its own micro-climate. Through local adaptations, people have met their needs generation after generation.

But all this has changed. The message being drummed into Third World populations is: "imported equals *good*, local equals *crap*" But what can work in a country like France or Britain will not work in countries like India or China. There are vast differences in the lifestyle, culture and just the number of people that live in these countries. This blind and senseless imposition of western systems is simply turning the situation from bad to worse. The current trajectory is likely to shatter the dreams of hundreds of millions of the residents to live the American dream. They are blissfully unaware that for Americans themselves, their dream has turned into a nightmare.

Then there is another problem, that of scarce and finite resources. Already the third world's claims on the earth's resources are becoming highly visible. For example, for China's 1.3 billion people, the American dream is fast becoming the Chinese dream. Already millions of Chinese are living like Americans—eating more meat, driving cars, traveling abroad, and otherwise spending their fast-rising incomes much as

Americans do. Although these U.S.-style consumers are only a small fraction of the population, China's consumption of resources has spiked alarmingly. To reach the U.S. 2004 meat intake of 125 kilograms per person, China's meat consumption would rise from the current 64 million tons to 181 million tons in 2031, or roughly four fifths of current world meat production of 239 million tons.

Lets have a look at some of the facts:

If China's annual growth were to level at 8% for 20 years, then in 2030, Chinese per capita income will equal that of US today. And if they consume the way US does today, then:

- In 2030, China's 1.46 billion people will need twice as much paper as is produced worldwide today (there go the world's forests).

- In 2030, if there are three cars for every four persons (as it is now in the U.S.), then China will have 1.1 billion cars (the world currently has 860 million).

- To provide roads/highways/parking for three cars, China would have to pave an area comparable to what it now plants in rice.

- By 2030, China would need 98 million barrels of oil per day (the world currently produces 85 million barrels per day, and may never produce more than that).

If the current Western economic model will not work for China; it will definitely not work for India which will have a larger population than China by 2030. And it will not work for the other 3 billion people in developing nations. And in a globalized world where we are all interconnected (depending on the same grain, steel, and oil), the model won't work for industrialized countries either.

Not to repeat but the point of this projection exercise is to learn what happens when a large segment of humanity moves quickly up the global economic ladder. The experience proves that the fossil-fuel-based, auto-centered, throwaway economy has never and will never be successful. By applying this failing model, we are simply putting the life of the world's 85% people in jeopardy who live in these developing countries.

Then there is this grave crisis of governance. Most third world nations are confronted by increasing poverty, illiteracy, population, environmental degradation, crime, corruption and social unrest. Liberalisation of economies and globalisation are often being projected as the panacea for all these problems. But these are having just the opposite effect.

The unbridled growth in industrial activity has led to disturbing consequences such as unprecedented movement of materials, damage to the environment, and global warming. Facing bankruptcy, the third world nations have opened their economies to the global market. Situation is turning from bad to worse as the so called progress emboldens faulty institutions of governance which foster corruption, wastage and exploitation.

The present state of affairs in the world has thrown up several questions concerning the very discipline of economics itself.

And because Western countries have got big, big skyscraper building and many motorcars, India has become victimized: "Oh, without this motorcar and without this skyscraper building, we are condemned." So they are trying to imitate. They have forgotten their own culture.

Unfortunately, they are all bereft of this knowledge, their own culture. There is a Bengali verse written by one poet, apanar dhana vilaya-diye bhiksa-mage parera dvare. They have lost their own culture; now they are begging from other countries.

—Srila Prabhupada (Lecture, Mayapur, February 28, 1976)

13.
Rise of Farcical Centralised Democracies
Colonial Ghost Still Rules

As we enter the twenty-first century, it is hard to imagine how just sixty years ago the world was dominated by mainly European empires. In 1921, 84 per cent of the surface of the earth had been colonized since the sixteenth century. There were as many as 168 colonies and though by the mid-1960s most colonies were, at least formally, independent, the experience of subsequent decades showed how much the ghost of colonization still loomed over the post-colonial world.

Most third world nations on attaining independence, retained the centralised, non-transparent and bureaucratised exploitative colonial institutions. The glitter of western economies stems from the relentless exploitation of these resource rich colonies for centuries altogether. From Africa alone, the transatlantic slave trade resulted in the transportation of perhaps eleven million Africans to the Americas between the sixteenth and nineteenth centuries.

The colonial intent was to plunder as much as possible while keeping the costs to a bare minimum. In British India, the centerpiece of Britain's colonial empire, the entire European population in 1921 amounted to just 156,500 (or 0.06 per cent) out of a total of over 250 million. This feat was accomplished by pursuing a unscrupulous policy of divide and rule with the help of local collaborators.

Then there was phenomenal cruelty to force the natives into submission. The routine British use of aircraft to both awe and bomb into submission rebellious Arab tribes in Iraq in the 1920s is an example.

Wealth transfer was a one way traffic. All the wealth went to England but nothing came back in return. Until relatively late in their history, colonial states had a poor record of investment with barely a tenth of total British overseas investment in the Victorian era going to the non-white colonies. India recorded no increase in its per capita income in 190 years of British rule, with the colonial regime operating a policy of deliberate neglect when it came to development. The widespread consequence of cheap colonialism was uneven development and wide disparities between small, more or less Westernized elites and the rest. In addition, the movement of labour between colonies to work in the plantation sector in particular introduced new social and economic divisions. In the course of the nineteenth and early twentieth centuries, hundreds of thousands of Indians were transported to British colonies in the Caribbean, as well as to Burma, Ceylon, Malaya, Fiji, South  Africa, Kenya, and Mauritius—a factor that contributed to ethnic political tensions in all these territories after they became independent.

Virtually all developing countries are in some sense post-colonial, though not necessarily in the same ways. The impact of colonialism was transformative rather than transitory. As well as reshaping economic and political forms, it also changed the way people, especially the educated, came to see the world

As power was handed over by the last British Governor of the Gold Coast, Kwame Nkrumah, Ghana's first leader, declared confidently, 'We have won independence and founded a modern state'. Yet less than a decade later, on the eve of losing power, Nkrumah's summed up his misgivings about the reality of independence in a book entitled *Neo-Colonialism*: 'The essence of neo-colonialism is that the State which is subject to it is, in theory, independent and has all the outward trappings of international sovereignty. In reality its economic system and thus its political policy is directed from outside' A quarter of a century later, one international relations theorist coined the phrase 'quasi-states' to describe the majority of post-colonial states.

These 'quasi-states' even after their so called independence, have continued to suffer from the problems of bureaucratic overheads, misuse of authority, wastage of resources and corruption and are no better off than when they were under colonial rule.

One such instance would be India in its post-independence era. The colonial plunder went on shamelessly for two centuries but it was not limited to that. They plundered the internal resources of the populace as well by the process of 'mind colonization'. The slavery was not only physical and financial but intellectual as well. So much so that after India gained independence, post-independence leaders, coloured by the ideas and institutions of Western colonialism largely ignored what were seen as the idiosyncratic views of Mahatma Gandhi, the revered father figure of the Indian independence movement. They preferred the familiar structures of the British Raj. The sad result was the continuation of colonial legacy, at times in its more hideous form. The brown British were to prove worse than the original white British.

And this brings us to the biggest loot ever in mankind's history, the looting of India by her leaders in the post independence era. Trillions of dollars were siphoned off and deposited in the safe heavens of Swiss banking systems while millions died of malnutrition and hunger back home.

Swiss Banking Association report. 2008, gives a break up of countrywise deposits. Here are the top 5 countries.

India—- $1,456 billion
Russia —$ 470 billion
UK ——-$390 billion
Ukraine – $100 billion
China ——$ 96 billion

Source: Swiss Banking Association report 2008

This is more money than all the money in all the banks in India taken together. There is more Indian money in Swiss banks than rest of the world combined.

Is India a poor country? An amount 13 times larger than the country's foreign debt stashed away in secret Swiss accounts, one needs to rethink if India is a poor country. This ill-begotten wealth is even higher than India's GDP and three times that of market capitalisation on national stock exchange.

Corrupt industrialists, politicians, bureaucrats, cricketers, film actors, sex trade and protected wildlife operators, to name just a few, are the accomplices in this historical heist. But this is just the story of Swiss bank accounts. What about other international banks?

By allowing the proliferation of tax havens in the twentieth century, the Western world explicitly encourages the movement of scarce capital from the developing countries to the rich.

With the Indo US Nuclear deal having been signed now, many think that it will create an unprecedented mother of all opportunities for many to add to this booty in Swiss Banks.

In March 2005, the Tax Justice Network (TJN) published a research finding demonstrating that $11.5 trillion of personal wealth was held offshore by rich individuals across the globe. The findings estimated that a large proportion of this wealth was managed from some 70 tax havens.

Further, augmenting these studies of TJN, Raymond Baker -- in his widely celebrated book titled Capitalism's Achilles Heel: Dirty Money and How to Renew the Free Market System -- estimates that at least $5 trillion have been shifted out of poorer countries to the West since the mid-1970s. It is further estimated by experts that one per cent of the world's population holds more than 57 per cent of total global wealth, routing it invariably through these tax havens. How much of this is from India is anybody's guess.

What is to be noted here is that most of the wealth of Indians parked in these tax havens is illegitimate money acquired through corrupt means. Naturally the secrecy associated with the bank accounts in such places is central to the issue, not their low tax rates as the term 'tax havens' suggests. Two decades ago, Bofors guns scandal rocked the nation and no one could trace the ultimate beneficiary of those transactions because of the secrecy associated with these bank accounts.

When plunder becomes a way of life for a group of men living together in society, they create for themselves in the course of time a legal system that authorizes it and a moral code that glorifies it. ~ *Frederic Bastiat*

14.

Modern Economics

Its All About Lying, Deceit And Propaganda

On January 7, 2009, India Inc. woke up to a shocker of a life time - $1.6 billion Satyam Computers fraud. Chairman Ramalinga Raju and his family cooked up books and siphoned off money in what is being termed as India's biggest corporate fraud to date. By the end of the day, the fourth largest IT company lost a staggering Rs 10,000 crore in market capitalisation as investors reacted sharply and dumped shares, leaving an uncertain future for the company and its 53,000 employees. The entire stock market crashed.

Satyam's balance sheet as on Sep 30, 2008, carried an inflated (nonexistent) cash and bank balances of Rs 5,040 crore (as against Rs 5,361 reflected in the books).

Satyam fraud clouds the corporate governance of India Inc. More skeletons came out from corporate closets and it posed a big question over the credibility of auditors in general also.

Ramesh Damani, a financial expert, was quoted as saying, "I am actually a little less surprised at what was going on because I have been in the markets long enough and know all manners of companies, not just in India but across the world, do some degree of cooking of books, and that is let's say 'accepted'."

Damani added, " In fact a survey in the US that was conducted a couple of years back of CFOs, 70% of the CFOs said that they had always been pressurised to cook the books by the CEO, and a reasonable proportion of the 70% admitted to having cooked the books. And that is the US. So, the fact is that companies cook books."

When asked whether market fears were legitimate that many more

companies were propping up their books if not cooking them, he replied, "It is a great question and if you ask me, off the record, I could name you 50 companies where I am not convinced about the quality of earnings coming through the reports that they do. Beginning this quarter, the market will examine, with a whole new microscope or a whole new magnifying glass, to see exactly what the quality of earnings is. Is it legitimate, is the bank balance legitimate, and there are lot of well-created, highly liquid counters where we always puzzle and scratch heads as to how they produce these results in an operating environment that is so non-conducive. Companies will inevitably have to face analysts who are more hostile, auditors who are more hostile, and inevitably, there will be a lot of companies that fall through the crack."

In year 2005, the American airlines Delta and Northwest's story was quite similar. The America's airline crisis took a stunning turn for the worse when Delta Air Lines Inc. and Northwest Airlines Corp. filed for bankruptcy in the face of massive losses in 2005.

Much of the problems of these airlines were caused by all the CFOs and MBAs hired to paint a rosy picture of earnings along with converting losses into profits through creative accounting.

The suited guys with absolutely no life experience, fresh off the MBA assembly line of Harvard are hired to replace the old-gen economists in the vain hope of increased efficiency.

> "*The best way to destroy the capitalist system is to debauch the currency. By a continuing process of inflation, governments can confiscate, secretly and unobserved, an important part of the wealth of their citizens.*"
> —*John Maynard Keynes*

Sure, it is all good, as long as the economy is coasting along. As soon as it hits a rough patch, it becomes necessary to lie, so that you may cover up the mess. And one lie leads to another, and another, and then the whole thing falls flat.

The stock markets are largely the outcome of manipulation, rumour-mongering and irrational exuberance. The gullible masses suffer when stock markets crash. Whole life savings of ordinary, hapless investors are wiped out in the wake of the financial meltdowns.

Karandhara: Yes. Whenever there is an economic depression, then gold remains valuable. Just like when the stock market crashed in 1929, if you had gold you could still purchase goods. No matter how bad the economy was, people would accept gold as barter, but not currency.

Prabhupada: Yes. Indian economy was that if you have got extra money, you get gold ornament for your wife. So then your money is stocked there. Or purchase some utensils, silver utensils. That was Indian economy. This depositing in the bank and thinking that I am getting good interest, that is another cheating. It is another cheating. If things are not available, what will you get by getting interest? Therefore I am advising that purchase land and produce our own food. There will be no problem.

Karandhara: The inflation rate is higher than the interest rate. If you earn 5 3/4 % interest in a year, the inflation has gone up 6% in a year. So actually your money, at best it's kept the same.

Prabhupada: The money is to be kept in cattle and grains. That is Indian economy, cattle and grains. If you have got many cows, you get milk. Milk preparation. And if you have got grain, then where is your problem? You prepare your foodstuff at home and eat and chant Hare Krsna. Where is your problem? You want to eat and live peacefully. So if you have got grains and milk, you have got enough food and there is no problem. You haven't got to go fifty miles for your work, and then you require a tin car. So many problems. But if you get your food at home, then eat them and chant Hare Krsna and go back to home, back to Godhead. Simple thing.

(Morning Walk, December 31, 1973, Los Angeles)

15.

Consumption Crazy Throwaway Economies

Overconsumption, like any general phenomenon, is multi-faceted and eludes precise definition. In a broad sense, we use or consume many kinds of things in our lives (air, water, electricity, wool, land, cotton, fertilizer, paper, chocolate, plastics, CFCs, graphite, fuel oil, food), and corporations "consume" many things in the production of goods and services for "consumers." Moreover, not all consumption degrades the environment. But a broad and growing literature strongly suggests that we are consuming in ways that are unhealthy for ourselves and unsustainable for our natural environment.

In general, overconsumption occurs where (1) people (individually or collectively) make consumption an end in itself, rather than a means to some higher human purpose, where (2) economic/ legal systems fail to follow free market principles, or where (3) the economic/legal system fails to adequately recognize and account for future costs, the interests of future generations, or finite limits to the use of natural resources as "capital."

We will look first at overconsumption in its first aspect, where consumption has become an end in itself. In fact, the illusions created by the corporate dream merchants have become the new religion. In feeding the dreams and desires of material salvation here and now, corporations have deliberately created "the consumer," an ideal marketing target who rejects tradition, focuses on immediate gratification, and is steeped in desire for all things new. Having more and newer things each year has become not just something we want but something we need. The idea of more, of ever increasing wealth, has become the center of our identity and our security, and we are caught by it as an addict by his drugs. This collective addiction is well-entrenched. When environmentalists claim that we need to reduce consumption, business and the consumer both recoil. By now the consumer is so well-conditioned to satisfying needs through things that any suggestion to cut back is met with "intense anxiety, depression, rage, and even panic."

In part this is because the average consumer is exposed to hundreds of advertisements each day, and the process begins at an early age. Even if the specific product is not remembered, the overall message is: there is a product to meet your every need, if only you will buy it. As Alan Durning has noted, "People actually remember few ads. Yet commercials have an effect nonetheless. Even if they fail to sell a particular product, they sell consumerism itself by ceaselessly reiterating the idea that there is a product to solve each of life's problems, indeed that existence would be satisfying and complete if only we bought the right things."

Advertisers thus cultivate needs by hitching their wares to the infinite yearnings of the human soul. As Kanner and Gomes point out, "large-scale advertising is one of the main factors in modern society that creates and maintains a peculiar form of narcissism ideally suited to consumerism. As such, it creates artificial needs within people that directly conflict with their capacity to form a satisfying and sustainable relationship with the natural world."

The irrational nature of this addictive consumption leads many of us to focus on the self to the exclusion of community. Even as the Gross Domestic Product (GDP) continues to rise, there is strong evidence of declining social welfare and large holes in the "moral fabric" of our society.

Several post-war institutions were established to keep the peace and establish commercial prosperity, including the World Bank, the IMF,

Be glad that you're greedy; the national economy would collapse if you weren't. — *Mignon McLaughlin*

the United Nations, and the General Agreement on Tariffs and Trade (GATT). The UN would keep the peace, the World Bank would work to bring developing economies into the international trading system, and free trade through GATT would reduce the likelihood of trade wars and, thus, reduce the likelihood of military conflict.

Yet in over fifty years since World War II, "development" and free trade have not brought economic or social well-being to much of the "developing" nations, and much of the blame can be placed squarely on industrialized nations that continue to command the lion's share of the world's resources for themselves.

In short, consumption has become an end in itself, rather than a means to individual enlightenment or happiness, or as a means to social justice, either domestically or globally. And as the consumption habit  becomes an end in itself, we have become blind to our own deeper needs. The entire creaking economy is based on a few ideas which no longer work:

-Create "aggregate demand" (i.e. consumer demand, which then creates business demand) and the economy "grows," people are hired and get paid, and that's good.

-When consumer demand slumps because people are over-indebted and can't afford to buy more of anything, then "stimulate" demand with massive Central State spending to replace the vanished private demand.

-Demand is endless. You can never have enough stuff, food, vacations, education, healthcare and toys. Give people free money, or the ability to borrow nearly-free money, and they will spend, spend, spend. This creates "growth" which is always good.

The Earth's resources are erroneously assumed to be infinite and inexhaustible. Even if not, we have faith that human ingenuity will find suitable substitutes for any shortages, and technological "fixes" for serious degradation of our natural environment.

The consumer-driven economy presumes that nations and corporations must grow in order to "progress," and assumes that the "rational economic person" will strive to amass as much material wealth and experience as much pleasure as possible. "You only go around once in life," one beer commercial used to implore, "So go for all the gusto you can!" These beliefs encourage overconsumption as a way of life, for they posit a world of boundless freedom without natural limits or moral restraints on human action.

Nearly 70 percent of world trade is controlled by just 500 corporations, and one percent of all multinationals own half the total stock of foreign direct investment. In short, a few MNCs are consolidating their hold on the global economy. Giving MNCs this kind of control over the global economy has repercussions for local economies. In both the U.S. and across the globe, many large corporations - either directly or through intermediaries - are creating barriers to entry, stifling local economies, and racing to liquidate finite resources.

Religion Promoting Crass Materialism And Feigned Penance

Religious preachers and ministries have promptly jumped on the corporate bandwagon in promoting consumerism. Simple living, austerity and frugality belong to a bygone era. Many ministries are thriving on the notion that increasing material well being is the Lord's 'fervent' wish for us all. In a similar vein, one recent book reassures us that God Wants You to be Rich. They propose that "Why would an awesome and mighty God want anything less for his children?"

All over the world, messiahs, messangers and holy men relaying the message of corporations rather than the message of God. In Bible, Jesus warns that each of his disciples may have to "deny himself" and even "take up his Cross." In support of this alarming prediction, he forcefully contrasts the fleeting pleasures of today with the promise of eternity: "For what profit is it to a man," he asks, "if he gains the whole world, and loses his own soul?" It is one of the New Testament's hardest teachings, yet generations of churchgoers have understood that being religious, on some level, means being ready to sacrifice--money, autonomy or even their lives.

But for a growing number of Christians, the question is better restated, "Why not gain the whole world plus my soul?" For several decades, a philosophy has been percolating that seems to turn the

The entire world economy rests on the consumer; if he ever stops spending money he doesn't have on things he doesn't need we're done for. -Bill Bonner

Gospels' passage on its head: certainly, it allows, the faithful should keep one eye on heaven. But the new good news is that God doesn't want us to wait. In a nutshell, it suggests that a God who loves you does not want you to be broke. In other words, go ahead, enjoy yourself and have a good life.

Method Behind The Madness - A History

Creating the culture of desire was not an overnight event. According to William Leach, much of the story of the big business is the story of how the giants of the late nineteenth and early 20th century took a land of spiritually oriented, frugal folk and "created a material culture of self-indulgence." Business became skilled in using colors, glass, and light to create exciting images of a this-world paradise conveyed by elegant models and fashion shows. Museums offered displays depicting the excitement of the new culture. Gradually, the individual was surrounded by messages reinforcing the culture of desire. Advertisements, department store show windows, electric signs, fashion shows, the sumptuous environments of leading hotels, and billboards all conveyed artfully crafted images of the good life. Credit programs made it seem effortless to buy that life.

Advertising gained considerable momentum after World War II, especially with the advent of television. The average adult in U.S. sees about 21,000 commercial messages a year; the largest 100 corporations in the U.S. pay for about 75 percent of commercial television time and about half the public television time. With advertising for a 30 second segment in prime time costing over $200,000 on television networks, only the largest corporations can afford it.

We are systematically stimulating the addictive, irrational impulse to feed a spiritual emptiness with more and more "goods."

As we near the end of this century, the "culture" of television has largely replaced community and family life, cultural pursuits, and reading. Coupled with big corporations' ability to influence the legal environment of business, corporate "freedom of speech" encourages a consumer-driven economy, with consumers perennially in pursuit of this year's "hottest buy."

16.

Ominous Headlines

Negative Headlines Spooking Investors, Markets Around Globe

The history is trying to repeat itself in last couple of years. Headlines are blaring - Financial markets in a free-fall, Chaos on Wall St, International markets in a tailspin, European bailout, More banks to fail, Investors shy away amidst growing fears, Congress approves bailout, 51 Million to loose jobs, China goes down in first quarter, U.S. downgrade heralds a new financial era, the world's leaders are terrifyingly out of their depth, etc etc.

These foreboding headlines are indications of something coming out way, if we are willing to listen. And its not just headlines but the public morale is also pretty low.

Despite rosy financial forecasts made by economists, public fears that the world is about to sink into another depression are reaching depressing extremes. A recent CNN poll reveals that nearly half of Americans believe a 1930s-scale depression is possible within the next 12 months. A whopping 19% of Americans believe it's "very likely" — the most since the economy tanked in the fall of 2008. An additional 29% said a depression is "somewhat likely." If we use the original Great Depression as a model, that means many of us are pondering 25% unemployment and rampant homelessness.

Well, more than the common man in the street, the world's leaders are terrifyingly out of their depth. Certain years have gone down in history as great global turning points, after which nothing was remotely the same: 1914, 1929, 1939, 1989. Now it looks horribly plausible that 2011 will join their number. The very grave financial crisis that has hung over the world ever since the banking collapse of three years ago has taken a sinister turn, with the most dreadful and sobering consequences. Emergency telephone conferences of the world's finance ministers is failing to yield any results.

There have been warnings that we may be in for a repeat of the calamitous events of 2008. The truth, however, is that the situation is potentially much bleaker even than in those desperate days. Back then, policy-makers had at their disposal a whole range of powerful tools to remedy the situation which are simply not available today.

First of all, the 2008 crisis struck at the ideal stage of an economic cycle. Interest rates were comparatively high. This meant that central banks were in a position to avert disaster by slashing the cost of borrowing. Today, rates are still at rock bottom, so that option is no longer available.

Second, the global situation was far more advantageous three years ago. One key reason why Western economies appeared to recover so fast was that China responded with a substantial economic boost. Today, China, plagued by high inflation as a result of this timely intervention, is in no position to stretch out a helping hand.

But it is the final difference that is the most alarming. Back in 2008, national balance sheets were in reasonable shape. In Britain, for example, state debt (according to the official figures, which were, admittedly, highly suspect) stood at around 40 per cent of GDP. This meant that they had the balance sheet strength to step into the markets and bail out failed banks. Partly as a result, national debt has now surged past the 60 per cent mark, meaning that it is impossible for the British

"Do you have any idea how cheap stocks are now? Wall Street is now being called Wal-Mart Street." —Jay Leno

government to perform the same rescue operation without risking bankruptcy. Many other Western democracies face the same problem.

The consequences are terrifying. Policy-makers find themselves in the position of a driver heading down the outside lane of a motorway who suddenly finds that none of his controls are working: no accelerator, no brakes and a faulty steering wheel. Experience, skill and a prodigious amount of luck are required if a grave accident is to be averted. Unfortunately, it is painfully apparent that none of these qualities are available: World leaders are out of their depth.

17.

Economic Gloom Descends On The World

A survey of 24 of the world's biggest economies, conducted by Ipsos MORI, a leading market research company in May 2011, placed Britain among the most negative countries, ranking alongside Italy and just above France and debt-laden Spain. Britain was among the world's gloomiest nations, with just one in ten people rating the economy as 'good', according to the poll.

In the survey, the Britons were equally pessimistic looking ahead, with only one in ten expecting their economy to strengthen in the next six months. Only the Japanese, who have seen their economy enter recession after an earthquake and tsunami, and the Hungarians were more negative. The citizens of bail-out recipients Ireland, Greece and Portugal were not polled.

Bobby Duffy, managing director of Ipsos MORI, feels the British gloom is understandable: "House prices are absurd and the cost of living is increasing rapidly in comparison to earnings. There is rightly a lot of pessimism out there, which will have an impact on growth."

Mood was better in Saudi Arabia, Sweden, India, China and Australia, where in each of them, at least seven in ten citizens thought that their economy was 'alright'. Germany just failed to make that grouping. Despite rosy financial forecasts made by many economists this spring, fears that many nations are about to sink into another depression are reaching depressing extremes.

However, everyone everywhere seems to agree on this point - there's now every possibility of the world slipping back into recession or even something worse. Governments are all out of ammunition and as the world economy once more heads towards the rocks, they appear out of ideas and options.

Rarely have economic policymakers seemed as devoid of solutions as they are in Washington in September 2011 for the annual meeting of the International Monetary Fund (IMF). After more than three years of crisis fighting, the language is again one of growing alarm and panic, but tinged with a war-weariness that doesn't bode well for the collective action needed to halt the slide back into recession.

"Time is running out", the IMF screams in its latest Global Financial Stability Report. "The set of policy choices that are both economically   viable   and politically feasible is shrinking as the crisis shifts into a new, more political phase". With the world economy once more approaching stall speed, Olivier

Blanchard, the IMF's chief economist, talks of being back in "the danger zone" and of the crisis again running out of control. It's hard to disagree.

The mood at the same event two years ago in Istanbul was greatly different. Then, finance ministers and central bankers were roundly congratulating themselves on having saved the world from a second Great Depression. They'd rescued the banking system, pump-primed national economies with fiscal stimulus and flooded the world with newly-printed money.

Economies were growing again and the crisis seemed to be over. There was a sense of having come through the worst and of entering a brave new world of renewal, lessons learned, reform and reflection. As is now painfully obvious, it was all ludicrously premature.

The solvency issue at the heart of the Western banking system wasn't solved at all, but merely papered over. The rapid bounce back in economic

No one is rich whose expenditures exceed his means, and no one is poor whose incomings exceed his outgoings."
— *Thomas C.Haliburton*

activity to pre-crisis levels hasn't occurred, and confidence plummeting to rock bottom.

Against this grim backdrop of negatives, the IMF announced a "call to arms". Christine Lagarde, the IMF's managing director says, "The collaborative spirit that prevailed at the height of the 2008 crisis, when countries came together to take collective action against the downturn, must be revived." Yet the sense of policy fatigue and indecision is palpable.

"We've already sent the best of our cavalry into battle, and it's come back in tatters. There's a limit to what more we can do."
—*An EU Minister on Eurozone crisis*

18.

Modern Economics

Failing To Increase Happiness

Since the time of Adam Smith, the wealth of nations has been used as a proxy for the well-being of nations. We measure whether life is getting better by checking whether the good numbers (GDP, personal incomes, and so on) are going up and the bad numbers (unemployment, inflation, and so on) are going down. However, over the past half century, something strange has happened. Many nations' per capita GDP - the value of all the goods and services a nation produces divided by its population - has gone up remarkably but the well-being hasn't budged. In many places people have grown richer but not one jot happier. There's ample evidence that in all postindustrial societies, material wealth and broader happiness are no longer closely in sync.

The standard approach of economics in minimizing costs and maximizing profits fails to satisfy the social necessities of a stable society, a sustainable ecological environment and the satisfaction of Greatest Happiness Principle (GHP).

Even in the West after two hundred years of the industrial revolution neither they could approached a communist paradise of affluence nor a capitalist society which guarantees welfare, happiness and well-being to the people. However, the emotional state of people feeling happy even under conditions of poverty is striking psychologists, sociologists and now even economists. By asking people repeatedly about their emotional state of mind and giving a self-assessment on the degree of their personal happiness they found out that happiness is only weakly linked towards material wealth after a certain standard of living has been accomplished.

Even if there are many unsolved research questions about - how to measure it? – there is sufficient empirical evidence that the link between material wealth accounted as personal disposable income does not have the strong correlation with the emotional states people declare as their happiness. This is also called Easterlin paradox, named after the economist Richard Easterlin. He asks, "Why at a point-in-time are happiness and income positively associated, but over the life-cycle there is no relation?" The Easterlin Paradox is a key concept in happiness economics. He discussed the factors contributing to happiness in the 1974 paper "Does Economic Growth Improve the Human Lot? Easterlin found that in international comparisons the average reported level of happiness does not vary much with national income per person, at least for countries with income sufficient to meet basic needs. Similarly, although income per person rose steadily in the United States between 1946 and 1970, average reported happiness showed no long-term trend and declined between 1960 and 1970.

The implication for government policy is that once basic needs are met, policy should focus not on economic growth or GDP, but rather on increasing life satisfaction or Gross national happiness (GNH).

An overall increasing volume of goods and services cannot increase overall happiness to a certain extent, given by the saturation level. Beyond this material wealth does not improve happiness anymore.

It is the problem of luxury consumption that it has insufficient leisure time at its disposal so that one cannot consume all the products which could be bought given one has sufficient wealth and income at ones disposal. Furthermore even owning the most expensive items cannot establish more happiness. The attempt to extract happiness from ever preposterous luxury items show clearly the dilemma. One simply often spends money on luxury items to impress others but much less so to derive direct happiness from it.

It is good to have money and the things that money can buy, but it's good too, to check up once in a while and make sure you haven't lost the things money can't buy.
—George Lorimer

One reason is that humans are creatures of comparison. Research shows that happiness levels depend inversely on the earnings levels of a person's neighbors. Prosperity next door makes you dissatisfied. It is relative income that matters: when everyone in a society gets wealthier, average well-being stays the same.

Therefore it directly points to happiness obtained from social relations and in particular the perception generated from others. To be part of a community, a family, groups with a particular social status, etc. are contributing to the happiness of an individual. Often people spend a lot of their income just to establish a position in a social network which they desire to belong to.

Research on happiness has become a highly debated research topic in the West over the last couple of years. Searching the IDEAS-database – database of research papers and publications in economics - for the keyword happiness, one ends up with more than 1000 hits.

This has not been the case ten years ago. The significant growth of income in the West over the last two centuries and in particular after WWII has led to new questions concerning the aims of economic activity. Furthermore the environmental crisis and the prospect of significant climate change caused by excessive use of global resources in particular of energy and natural resources point again towards the need not to exhaust the resource base. Limits towards resource based growth become a key concern in the global policy agenda. If economic well-being would be intrinsically connected towards energy and resource based growth than sooner or later economics would face a crisis.

Well known economists have started to ask themselves and their profession: Would You Be Happier If You Were Richer? This might seem obscure for many outsiders because many people think that economics is just about how to get rich and wealthy. However, there is an increasing discomfort emerging that the continuous striving for greater

Just like here you see in Europe, America. They have got the high standard of life, they have got skyscraper buildings, very big, big roads, motorcars. But what is that? Simply struggling. Are they happy?
—*Srila Prabhupada (Lecture, Srimad-Bhagavatam, Vrndavana, December 7, 1975)*

material wealth does not emotionally make most people to feel that they are better off.

People in poor countries are often more optimistic than those in rich societies. The Pew survey finds that optimism – as defined by the difference between where people place themselves on the ladder of life today compared with where they think they will be in five years – is up in Africa and in Latin America over the last five years. By comparison, optimism is down in Western Europe, Canada and the United States. These findings broadly track with recent surveys in 11 African countries by the Afrobarometer that found unusually high levels of optimism among the poorest and most insecure people.

Psychologists of the West can tell a lot of stories about the neurosis of people facing little or no material shortcomings, feel emotionally dissatisfied, lonely and lack a direction of life. Having accomplished material well-being obviously does not lead to greater happiness in the end.

Well, its true. In a report published on September 5, 2011 by Hans Ulrich Wittchen, director of the institute of clinical psychology and psychotherapy at Germany's Dresden University, it was reported that Europeans are plagued by mental and neurological illnesses, with almost 165 million people or 38 per cent of the population suffering each year from a brain disorder such as depression, anxiety, insomnia or dementia. This large study noted that mental disorders have become Europe's largest health challenge of the 21st century.

Its the same situation in America. In any given year 26 percent of American adults suffer from mental disorders, based on guidelines in the official handbook for diagnosing mental illness.

According to a 2005 survey by the National Institute of Mental Health, rate of mental illness is 'staggering'. Many of these cases go untreated.

Anybody who thinks money will make you happy, hasn't got money.
— David Geffen

A World Health Organization study in 2004, published in an issue of The Journal of the American Medical Association, shows that rates of most mental illness are far higher in the U.S. than in any other country in the world.

Overall, the survey of more than 60,000 adults in 14 countries showed a 27% rate of mental disorders in the U.S. population for a list of diseases. That list includes: depression, anxiety, eating disorders, and substance abuse. The U.S. rate was substantially higher than that of any other country measured, including other industrialized nations such as Belgium, which showed a 12% illness rate.

Despite evidence that one in four U.S. adults experiences mental illness at some point, researchers still consider the figure an underestimate. They acknowledge that many people remain reluctant to tell surveyors about their mental health history, mainly because of the stigma attached to mental diseases.

Ronald C. Kessler, PhD, a professor of health care policy at Harvard Medical School says, "These numbers are absolutely staggering. When we get to the bottom of the situation, my guess is it is going to be doubly staggering."

19.

Modern Economics - Of the 1%, by the 1%, for the 1%

Founded on Principles of Injustice And Inequality

While booming stock markets, giant mergers and frantic financial speculation provide huge rewards to a tiny minority, the majority of the world's people are not enjoying much benefit from the neoliberal system of growth and development. For many, in fact, living standards have stagnated or declined, while the burden of work and insecurity have grown.

World Is Heading Toward "Grotesque Inequalities"

Almost half the world — over three billion people — live on less than $2 a day while 1.3 billion get by on less than $1 per day. At least 80% of humanity lives on less than $10 a day.

More than 80 percent of the world's population lives in countries where income differentials are widening.

The United Nations Development Program (UNDP) reported in 1998 that the world's 225 richest people now have a combined wealth of $1 trillion. That's equal to the combined annual income of the world's 2.5 billion poorests people.

The wealth of the three most well-to-do individuals now exceeds the combined GDP of the 48 least developed countries.

The GDP (Gross Domestic Product) of the 41 Heavily Indebted Poor Countries (567 million people) is less than the wealth of the world's 7 richest people combined.

While global GNP grew 40 percent between 1970 and 1985 (suggesting widening prosperity), the number of poor grew by 17 percent.

Although 200 million people saw their incomes fall between 1965 and 1980, more than 1 billion people experienced a drop from 1980 to 1993.

Number of children in the world are 2.2 billion. Out of that 1 billion live in abject poverty. (every second child)

In sub-Saharan Africa, twenty nations remain below their per capita incomes of two decades ago while among Latin American and Caribbean countries, eighteen countries are below their per capita incomes of ten years ago.

UNDP reported in 1996 that 100 countries were worse off than 15 years ago.

Three decades ago, the people in well-to-do countries were 30 times better off than those in countries where the poorest 20 percent of the world's people live. By 1998, this gap had widened to 82 times (up from 61 times since 1996).

Rural areas account for three in every four people living on less than US$1 a day and a similar share of the world population suffering from malnutrition. However, urbanization is not synonymous with human progress. Urban slum growth is outpacing urban growth by a wide margin.

Approximately half the world's population now live in cities and towns. In 2005, one out of three urban dwellers (approximately 1 billion people) was living in slum conditions.

In 1998, that 20 percent of the world's people living in the highest-income countries accounted for 86 percent of total private consumption expenditures while the poorest 20 percent accounted for only 1.3 percent. That's down from 2.3 percent three decades ago.

Seventy percent of those living on less than $1 per day are women. With global population expanding 80 million per year, World Bank President James D. Wolfensohn cautions that, unless we address "the challenge of inclusion," 30 years hence we will have 5 billion people living on less than $2 per day.

"In a country well governed, poverty is something to be ashamed of. In a country badly governed, wealth is something to be ashamed of."
— *Confucius (Chinese philosopher, 551-479 BC)*

Two billion people worldwide now suffer from anemia, including 55 million in industrial countries. Given current trends in population growth and prosperity-hoarding, three decades from now we could have a world in which 3.7 billion people are anemic.

These related phenomena led UN development experts to observe that the world is heading toward "grotesque inequalities," concluding: "Development that perpetuates today's inequalities is neither sustainable nor worth sustaining."

UNDP calculates that an annual 4 percent levy on the world's 225 most well-to-do people (average 1998 wealth: $4.5 billion) would suffice to provide the following essentials for all those in developing countries: adequate food, safe water and sanitation, basic education, basic health care and reproductive health care. At present, 160 of those individuals live in OECD countries; 60 reside in the United States.

As of 1995, Federal Reserve research found that the wealth of the top one percent of Americans is greater than that of the bottom 95 percent. Three years earlier, the Fed's Survey of Consumer Finance found that the top one percent had wealth greater than the bottom 90 percent.

In 1997, 1.4 million Americans filed for personal bankruptcy. That works out to roughly 7,000 bankruptcies per hour, 8 hours a day, 5 days a week.

Between 1970 and 1990, the typical American worked an additional 163 hours per year. That's equivalent to adding an additional month of work per year - for the same or less pay.

The combined net worth of the Forbes 400 was $738 billion on September 1, 1998. That's up from $624 billion in 1997. That's an average one-year increase of $285 million per person. That works out to $780,000 per day or $32,500 per hour ($541 per second).

Microsoft CEO Bill Gates has more wealth than the bottom 45 percent of American households combined.

Spending on luxury goods grew by 21 percent from 1995 to 1996 while overall merchandise sales grew only 5 percent.

For every $1 in aid a developing country receives, over $25 is spent on debt repayment.

In 1960, the 20% of the world's people in the richest countries had 30 times the income of the poorest 20% — in 1997, 74 times as much.

In the last 20 years in the US, 56 percent of all income gains went to the top 1 percent of wealthy Americans, and more than a third went to the top one-tenth of one percent.

Increases in executive compensation in recent decades have been spectacular. CEOs of the largest U.S. companies, for example, earned 42 times as much as the average worker as recently as 1980, but by 2001, they were earning more than 500 times as much.

The chief executives and top managers of the financial companies and MNCs are drawing fabulous salaries, bonuses and incentive payments which have no relation to the profit of the company. Horrific stories of their drawing astronomical payments running into millions of dollars and maintaining lavish lifestyles with private jets and palatial villas at exotic holiday destinations, appear in the press everyday. The bankers and fund mangers are not doing anything useful, they are simply shuffling money around to nobody's profit but their own. It is pure greed that is driving top corporate managers with disastrous consequences for the world economy.

There is no scarcity in this world. Its just a question of misallocation and mismanagement.

Consider the global priorities in spending in 1998

Global Priority	$U.S. Billions
Cosmetics in the United States	8
Ice cream in Europe	11
Perfumes in Europe and the United States	12
Pet foods in Europe and the United States	17
Business entertainment in Japan	35
Cigarettes in Europe	50
Alcoholic drinks in Europe	105
Narcotics drugs in the world	400
Military spending in the world	780

And compare that to what was estimated as additional costs to achieve universal access to basic social services in all developing countries:

Global Priority	$U.S. Billions
Basic education for all	6
Water and sanitation for all	9
Reproductive health for all women	12
Basic health and nutrition	13

(Source: The state of human development, United Nations Human Development Report 1998, Chapter 1, p.37)

India's 'Development' - A Case Study

Since post independence liberalisation of the economy, India has been blindly imitating the Western economic model. As a result the benefit of economic growth has been cornered by a small minority who lead an opulent lifestyle, while the vast majority continue to live in abject poverty and deprivation. According to Forbes, the number of billionaires in India doubled to 52 in 2009, their combined net worth reached $ 276 billion or a quarter of the country's GDP. As per data in the UNDP's Human Development Report (2007-08), while the poorest 10 per cent had three per cent share of the national income, the richest 10 per cent enjoyed a disproportionate 31 per cent share. Studies by ADB show that the disparity in income has been increasing over the last two decades. The National Commission for Enterprises in Unorganised Sector (NCEUS), chaired by  Arjun Sengupta, has found that 836 million Indians are poor and vulnerable, living on less than Rs 20 (40 cents) per day and have hardly experienced any improvement in their living standard since the early 1990s.

What can Rs 20 possibly fetch? For 836 million Indians, Rs 20 per day, or Rs 600 a month, buys them their daily sustenance.

Technically, a large chunk of these 836 million Indians 77 per cent of the country's population are above the poverty line at Rs 12 per day. But the reality is that they remain dismally poor according to the report on Conditions of Work and Promotion of Livelihood in the Unorganised Sector.

Published in 2007, this was the first authoritative study on the state of informal or unorganised employment in India, compiled by the National Commission for Enterprises in the Unorganised Sector (NCEUS), a government-affiliated body.

The report is based on government data for the period between 1993-94 and 2004-05.

A staggering 394.9 million workers, or 86 per cent of India's working population, toil in the unorganised sector, which means they work without a social security cover. Nearly 80 per cent of these workers are among those who live on less than Rs 20 per day.

Agriculture, the report found, was a fertile ground for poverty, especially for small and marginal farmers, 84 per cent of whom spent more than they earned and were often caught in debt traps.

Shameless Planning Commissions

In September 2011, in an affidavit before the Supreme Court the Planning Commission said that an individual income of just Rs. 25 (50 cents) a day constitutes adequate "private expenditure on food, education and health."

The affidavit bases its assertion on the findings of the Suresh Tendulkar Committee, which pegged the poverty line at Rs. 447 ($10) a month, or about Rs. 15 (30 cents) a day, at 2004-2005 prices.

Experts reacted with dismay to the affidavit. National Advisory Council member Aruna Roy said it reflected the government's lack of empathy for the poor. "This extremely low estimated expenditure is aimed at artificially reducing the number of persons Below the Poverty Line and thus reduce government expenditure on the poor," she alleged.

The shameless committee said its "proposed poverty lines have been validated by checking the adequacy of actual private expenditure per capita near the poverty lines on food, education and health by comparing them with normative expenditures consistent with nutritional, education and health outcomes."

This is the outcome of the decades of 'development and progress' and scams and squanderings. Shameless 'planning' commission members, living on fat salaries and sitting in plush offices, can hardly be more insensitive and insensible. They have overlooked the fact that trillions are stashed away in foreign accounts and trillions are being wasted in useless games and swallowed in scams while millions are starving.

China - Inequality And Social Unrest

China is faced with similar dilemma. While many Chinese - particularly on the coast and in the capital of Beijing - have seen a quantum leap forward in their way of life, the vast majority - perhaps some 800 million - have seen virtually no improvement in their agrarian lifestyle. Economic reform has raised incomes for many, making some phenomenally wealthy but scores of millions still remain mired in deep poverty. As China's export-dependant economy comes to a grinding halt in the midst of a worldwide recession, societal fissures are already beginning to develop or intensify which could lead to violence and possibly threaten the regime's stability. This growing gulf and breeding resentment may prompt broader class conflict. This is prompting government authorities to tighten controls over the internet as public anger mounts over inequality and official corruption.

With more than half a billion Chinese now online, authorities in Beijing are concerned about the power of the Internet to influence public opinion in a country that maintains tight controls on its traditional media outlets.

China's massive economic-stimulus program has supported near double-digit growth, but also stoked inflation, piled up debt and fueled another unwelcome development: social unrest.

According of Professor Sun Liping of Tsinghua University, in 2010, China was rocked by 180,000 protests, riots and other mass incidents—more than four times the tally from a decade earlier.

A sweeping monetary stimulus in 2009 and 2010—with the banks issuing 17.5 trillion yuan ($2.7 trillion) in new loans—translated into higher levels of inflation, reflected largely in food prices. In 2011, the problem has become more severe. The latest data show food prices rose 13.4% year-to-year in August.

The recent violence in China has exposed the limits of the government's ability to control the urban population using a sophisticated array of tools from Internet censorship to surveillance—part of what party leaders refer to as "social management." There is no doubt these are sensitive times in China. The country faces immense social and economic challenges.

"If a rich man is proud of his wealth, he should not be praised until it is known how he employs it."
—Socrates (Ancient Greek Philosopher, 470 BC-399 BC)

20.
Further Inadequacies And Defects
of Modern Economics

Modern economics has been said to be the most scientific of all the social sciences. Indeed, priding themselves on their scientific methodology, economists take only measurable quantities into consideration. Some even assert that economics is purely a science of numbers, a matter of mathematical equations. In its efforts to be scientific, economics ignores all non-quantifiable, abstract values.

But by considering economic activity in isolation from other forms of human activity, modern economists have fallen into the narrow specialization characteristic of the industrial age. In the manner of specialists, economists try to eliminate all non-economic factors from their considerations of human activity and concentrate on a single perspective, that of their own discipline.

While economic thinking has been in existence since the time of Plato and Aristotle, the study of economics has only really crystallized into a science in the industrial era. Like other sciences in this age of specialization, economics has become a narrow and rarefied discipline; an isolated, almost stunted, body of knowledge, having little to do with other disciplines or human activities.

Ideally, the sciences should provide solutions to the complex, interrelated problems that face humanity, but cut off as it is from other disciplines and the larger sphere of human activity, economics can do little to ease the ethical, social and environmental problems that face us today. And given the tremendous influence it exerts on our market-driven societies, narrow economic thinking may, in fact, be the primary cause of some of our most pressing social and environmental troubles.

Like other sciences, economics strives for objectivity. In the process, however, subjective values, such as ethics, are excluded. With no consideration of subjective, moral values, an economist may say, for instance, that a bottle of whiskey and a plate of salad have the same economic value, or that drinking in a night club contributes more to the economy than listening to a religious talk or volunteering for humanitarian work.

But the objectivity of economics is shortsighted. Economists look at just one short phase of the natural causal process and single out the part that interests them, ignoring the wider ramifications. Thus, modern economists take no account of the ethical consequences of economic activity. Neither the vices associated with the frequenting of night clubs, nor the wisdom arising from listening to a religious teaching, are its concern.

But is it in fact desirable to look on economics as a science? Although many believe that science can save us from the perils of life, it has many limitations. Science shows only one side of the truth, that which concerns the material world. By only considering the material side of things, the science of economics is out of step with the overall truth of the way things are. Given that all things in this world are naturally interrelated and interconnected, it follows that human problems must also be interrelated and interconnected. One-sided scientific solutions are bound to fail, and the problems bound to spread.

The global social and environmental crisis looming more and more at the horizon demand for a better analytical framework which would embed different aspects of human well being like social networks, environmental sustainability and psychological and spiritual well-being into the common microeconomic framework.

Economics is extremely useful as a form of employment for economists. —John Kenneth Galbraith

21.
Economics Without A Human Face
Killing Human Soul, Destroying Environment - Internal and External

Civilization is dying. The very notion of civilization is dead. Money has taken over. Honesty is the best policy - of course when there is money in it. Money is the modern God and greed is his religion. Benjamin Franklin was right in saying 'one who is of the opinion money will do everything may well be suspected of doing everything for money.'

India's Holy text, Srimad Bhagavatam foresaw this phenomenon five thousand years ago, "In Kali-yuga, wealth alone will be considered the sign of a man's good birth, proper behavior and fine qualities. And law and justice will be applied only on the basis of one's power. (SB 12.2.2)

Maximizing profit is the only real goal and people and the planet are out of the picture. The Free Market juggernaut crushes everything in its way. That's what it was invented for and fascism is the name of the game. The lawless chaos is hidden behind a screen of secrecy and lies..and propaganda.

Walter Williams, an economics professor, in his essay 'The Virtue of Greed' maintains that without greed, our current economic and social structures would implode. He echoes the view of many economists in saying 'greed produces preferable economic outcomes most times and under most conditions'.

Purposeless Life

When we salute all-consuming modern economy as the standout 'growth engine' of the world, we are in many ways paying tribute to the economic wonders of greed. But producing things, buying things and selling things is not the goal of life. This is not the purpose of life.

Human life is not meant for 'shopping culture' but for cultivation of 'spiritual culture'. Material things don't bring peace and happiness. Today billions of people have got things which even Kings did not have in the past. Car, computer, television, fridge, telephone - no king ever had these things but people are still restless and unhappy, more than ever before.

More For Me - The Modern Mantra

Resource depletion originates from a degraded self-centered mentality of me and mine. On individual, social and national level, more than ever before, we have become self-centered. President Bush was more concerned with the cough of his dog than the death of a million Iraqis. This phenomenal selfishness, apathy and unconcern is responsible for uneven distribution of resources and irresponsible exploitation of the same.

"The richest billion people in the world have created a form of civilization so acquisitive and profligate that the planet is in danger," says Alan Durning of the Worldwatch Institute. "The life-style of this top echelon car drivers, beef eaters, soda drinkers, and throwaway consumers-constitutes an ecological threat unmatched in severity."

For lot many people today, the world is shrinking to within themselves. Care and concern for others, even own family members and friends seems to be evaporating. More for me is the mantra or the guiding principle in life and let the world go to hell. The younger generation is confined to cell-phones and internet and they are living in a phantasmagoria, with very little touch of ground realities of life. It appears that a whole generation is simply floating in air and they suffer nervous breakdown when they come crashing on the ground. Other than

It seems to be a law in American life that whatever enriches us anywhere except in the wallet inevitably becomes uneconomic."
—*Russell Baker*

technology, things like fine arts, poetry, culture, spirituality, community life, contemplation, introspection etc. seem to have lost relevance. Materialism is commanding more attention than ever before and preoccupation with latest trends and fashions is sapping the vital energy.

Clinical psychologist Oliver James claims in his new book 'The Selfish Capitalist: Origins of Affluenza', that "selfish capitalism" is making us sick, literally. Owning too much stuff drives us into a spiral of sadness. He says the emergence of selfish capitalism has led to a "startling increase in the incidence of mental illness".

In Greed We Trust - Corruption & Loss of Integrity

The history of corruption goes back to the history of civilization. Although corruption exists in all societies and all times, the problem seems to be more prominent in the context of modern civilization.

Moreover, gradually corruption is becoming more and more institutionalised involving policy-making authorities. Colonial and neo-colonial backgrounds of a large number of present day developing countries had also contributed in flourishing corrupt practices.

With passage of time the concept has widened significantly. In modern world, corruption is evident in every sphere of life. Political corruption (involving governments or the policy-making bodies of a country) seems to be the major concern of developing countries whereas Corporate corruption is increasingly becoming a problem in industrialised rich nations. A long list of activities that include taking bribes, neglect of duties, profiteering activities, lavish living, gambling and visiting prostitutes, smuggling and so on can be included in the definition of corruption.

The political corruption has become so widespread that certain practices are no longer considered as illegal or unethical. Political donation at election times with expectations of favour in future is one of the most common practices in all democratic systems in the world.

In some nations, the corruption is as basic as greasing the palms of a telephone company clerk to expedite installation of a phone line or get away from violation of traffic laws. In other cases, corruption means millions in payoffs, often to secret foreign-bank accounts, where development funds are siphoned that should have been used to expedite roads, schools, bridges or basic health and sanitary facilities. Also if you get caught accepting bribe by anti-corruption bureau, you can get away by paying bribe.

Corruption occurs in all countries, irrespective of whether they are rich or poor, socialist or capitalist, dictatorship or democracies etc. Only the form of corruption and its extent might be different.

The corruption issue assumed a very serious dimension with technological development in early 1980s and with globalisation of production factors. From late 1980s it has become a very serious global issue.

Overspending & Indebtedness

On the surface, we seem better off than earlier generations. We might live more comfortable and stuff-filled lives than our forefathers did, but Oliver James, a Clinical psychologist, believes the rise of materialism has come with a high price tag attached - widespread anxiety and depression.

In the past, having a TV was seen as an indicator of wealth and class. Now, according to a study carried out by marketing and information group CACI, the average UK home has 4.7 television sets. Also, seven out of 10 children have a TV in their rooms and half of them have a DVD player too.

Can it really be the case that as we've become more comfortable, we've also become mentally ill? Yes, unfortunately it is the case. Average person's 'real' wage has broadly remained the same since the 1970s, he or she is now constantly bombarded with messages to buy, buy, buy, and aspire to a Posh and high flying life.

The media, advertising, reality TV shows and so on, they give people unrealistic aspirations that they simply cannot meet with their wages and living standards. As a result, people get sucked into competitiveness and workaholism....and indebtedness.

People end up tirelessly striving for material wealth and valuing it over family and friendships. This really heaps pressure on people, damaging their health.

Yet consumerism can be seriously addictive for some. Some experts believe 10% of Men and possibly 20% of British and American women,

Technological revolution that we witnessed in the last century has gone so far for our human moral to catch up with.
—Hun Sen

are manic, compulsive shoppers whose condition can lead to family breakups, depression and in some instances suicide. Rest of the world is trying to walk in their footsteps. An American pharmaceutical firm is developing a pill to help wean shopaholics off their addiction.

In a book titled Stop Me Because I Can't Stop Myself, a compulsive shopper called "Gloria" describes how she shopped online for six to eight hours a day, ending up in $80,000 of debt. She lost her job and split from her husband and checked into a psychiatric institution after "shopping ruined my family".

Debt is a serious problem not only for the individuals but for the nations as well. Between 1976 and 2009, the US external debt rose 137 times, whereas the GDP rose 14 times. There are 1.2 billion credit cards in the US, which have run up a debt of $2.5 trillion.

It is time we valued what is truly important rather than focusing society around competitiveness and consumption.

Social And Cultural Collapse Leads To Economic Collapse

Mr S. Gurumurthy, an economic thinker, has traced the 2008 financial crisis to the social and cultural collapse of the US, as a result of which it was transformed from the largest investor and lender in the world in 1976 to the biggest borrower today.

He emphasises that the 55 per cent divorce rate for first marriages in the US is playing a key role in the decline of family savings from a level of 70 per cent of national savings in 1974 to negative levels at present. It is a cultural shift from a saving to a spending economy.

Families are bankrupted and made government-dependent. The state takes over the functions of the family. As a result, 40 per cent of US GDP is accounted for by social security. In 2010-11, withdrawals for social securities were more than deposits" from taxes. This is the plight of the US economy. It has now turned into the largest welfare-state in the world.

According to Gurumurthy, this is how Modern Economics works –
-Atomize the individual (decouple man and woman by individualism).
-Dismember families (and orphan the children).
-Nationalize families and their functions (law and social security).

-Privatize the state and its functions.

-And finally, globalize the corporates.

This way, entire process of social evolution is put on reverse gear and the harmony between the individual, family and community and the larger society inter se and also between the society and the state is disturbed

Western Economic Model Unsustainable

"The crisis for workers is not over. With 200 million people unemployed and another 1.5 billion in precarious work, the crisis is not over for most people. Unless this social crisis is addressed further Jasmine Revolutions beckon. The West and East are working for some but not for all. The Western economic model that we've seen of this reliance on the market has failed. We need a new inclusive model of economic development. It is unsustainable."

— Philip Jennings, UNI General Secretary (the trade union message to the World Economic Forum (WEF) in Davos, Switzerland, telling CEOs and world leaders, 01/26/2011)

22.

Modern Economics - Dependent on War And Violence Death And Destruction

War - A Fall out of Economic Collapse

An economic collapse is a devastating breakdown of a national, regional, or territorial economy. It is essentially a severe economic depression characterised by a sharp increase in bankruptcy and unemployment. A full or near-full economic collapse is often quickly followed by months, years, or even decades of economic depression, social chaos, and civil unrest. Such crises have both been seen to afflict capitalist market economies and state controlled economies.

Today's economic climate feels like the summer of 1931. Economic gloom is descending on the world. The global currency system is breaking down. No world leader seems able to discern the problem, let alone forge a solution. The International Monetary Fund has abdicated into schizophrenia. All these does not forebode well for an already unstable world

Historically, the causes for war have always been economic in nature, no matter what the official reasons were. Economic disintegration and war go hand in hand, as both have a similar, imperial root.

If world economies continue to disintegrate and fall apart, war would

Is there any man, is there any woman, let me say any child here that does not know that the seed of war in the modern world is industrial and commercial rivalry?
— *Woodrow Wilson*

be a real threat. History is a witness that Bucks have been the basis of the great wars. Two world wars were fought to counteract British colonialism and their financial exploitation of the whole world. Hilter termed the British as a 'Shopkeepers' nation." The Germans made better and cheaper products but all the world markets were forcefully occupied by the British. This led to two great wars of the 20th century.

Modern word for unscrupulous colonials is corporations. Corporatisation is the modern way of colonizing the world. Today's world is getting ground under the corporate jackboot. These huge corporations make obscene profits from human misery and they want the world to remain in misery. They run our health care industry. They run our oil and gas companies. They run our bloated weapons industry. They run Wall Street and the major investment firms. They run our manufacturing firms. They also, ominously, run our government. World is simply not a safe place in the shadows of these greedy monsters. They want profits - when economy thrives and they want profits - when economy dies. Profits in a dying economy means war. Thats the only way to go about it.

The Stockholm International Peace Research Institute estimates that in 2007 military expenditures for the world were $1,339,000,000,000.

According to the Global Peace Index, indeed some $2.4 trillion or 4.4%, of the global economy is dependent on violence, referring to industries that create or manage violence - or the defense industry.

Emergence of Permanent War Economies

Wars always existed in human society but for thousands of years the methodology of war practically remained the same. It was a part time activity at best.

Paraphernalia of war was produced by decentralised small scale industries but these industries also had practical peacetime applications. For example, industries making swords in times of war could make

What is the advancement over the dogs? This destruction of another nation by nuclear bombs is the dogs' mentality. Sometimes, even when chained by their respective masters, two dogs will fight as soon as they meet. Have you seen it? It's no better than that.

—*Srila Prabhupada (Lecture, Melbourne, Australia)*

plowshares in times of peace. It was not until the late 19th to early 20th century that military weaponry became so complex as to require a large subset of industry dedicated solely to its procurement. Firearms, artillery, steamships, and later aircraft and nuclear weapons were markedly different from their ancient predecessors.

These newer, more complex weapons required highly specialized labor, knowledge and machinery to produce. The time and supporting industry necessary to construct weapon systems of increasing complexity and massive integration, made it no longer feasible to create assets only in times of war. Instead, nations dedicated portions of their economies for the full time production of war assets. The increasing reliance  of military on industry gave rise to a stable partnership—the military–industrial complex.

At the close of World War II, many countries did not return to a civilian economy, but kept to a 'permanent war economy.' The term 'permanent war economy' refers to the economic component within the military-industrial complex whereby the collusion between militarism and war profiteering are manifest as a permanently subsidised industry. Today the world retains the character of a global war economy; even in peacetime, with massive military expenditure.

The Runaway Military Budgets

Summarizing some key details from the Stockholm International Peace Research Institute (SIPRI)'s recent trends summary:
- World military expenditure in 2010 is estimated to have reached $1.62 trillion in current dollars;
- This represents a 50 per cent increase since 2001;
- This corresponds to 2.6 per cent of world gross domestic product (GDP), or approximately $236 for each person in the world; The United Nations and all its agencies and funds spend about $30 billion each

"We can do without butter, but, despite all our love of peace, not without arms. One cannot shoot with butter, but with guns." —Joseph Goebbels, German Minister of Propaganda

year, or about $4 for each of the world's inhabitants. This is a very small sum compared to most government budgets and it is less than three percent of the world's military spending.

The UN was set up to be committed to preserving peace through international cooperation and collective security. Yet, the UN's entire budget is just a tiny fraction of the world's military expenditure, approximately 1.8%. This goes to show that the world can spend so much on their military but contribute so little to the goals of global security, international cooperation and peace.

The USA with its massive spending budget, is the principal determinant of the current world trend, and its military expenditure now accounts for just under half of the world total, at 43% of the world total.

Increased Spending Even During Global Economic Crisis
Seeing The World Through The Lens of Threats

Both geopolitical hostilities and domestic violence tend to flare up during downturns.

The global financial and economic crisis has resulted in many nations cutting back on all sorts of public spending and yet military spending seems to be increasing.

According to SIPRI, the massive increase in US military spending has been one of the factors contributing to the deterioration of the US economy since 2001 and in addition to its direct impact of high military expenditure, there are also indirect and more long-term effects.

The lion's share of this money is not spent by the Pentagon on protecting American citizens. It goes to supporting U.S. military activities, including interventions, throughout the world. Were this budget and the organization it finances called the "Military Department," then attitudes might be quite different. Americans are willing to pay for defense, but they would probably be much less

Néstor Kirchner, the former President of Argentina claims that the former US President George W. Bush told him "The best way to revitalize the economy is war, and the U.S. has grou stronger with war."

willing to spend billions of dollars if the money were labeled "Foreign Military Operations."

Washington needs to make sure that the United States does not fall into the imperial trap of every other superpower in history, spending greater and greater time and money and energy stabilizing disorderly parts of the world on the periphery, while at the core its own industrial and economic might is waning.

US cost of war in the last one decade alone has been $3.7 trillion and counting.

Those numbers will continue to soar when considering often overlooked costs such as long-term obligations to wounded veterans and projected war spending from 2012 through 2020. The estimates do not include at least $1 trillion more in interest payments coming

The part of the American economy that's still booming.

due and many billions more in expenses that cannot be counted, according to the study.

In human terms, 224,000 to 258,000 people have died directly from warfare, including 125,000 civilians in Iraq. Many more have died indirectly, from the loss of clean drinking water, healthcare, and nutrition. An additional 365,000 have been wounded and 7.8 million people have been displaced.

Questions are being raised as to what the United States gained from its multitrillion-dollar investment.

"Every gun that is made, every warship launched, every rocket fired signifies, in the final sense, a theft from those who hunger and are not fed, those who are cold and are not clothed. The world in arms is not spending money alone. It is spending the sweat of its laborers, the genius of its scientists, the hopes of its children... This is not a way of life at all, in any true sense. Under the cloud of threatening war, it is humanity hanging from a cross of iron."
—Dwight D. Eisenhower, Former U.S. President, April 16, 1953

Third World Military Spending Soars to Dizzying Heights

"In 2002, arms deliveries to Asia, the Middle East, Latin America, and Africa constituted 66.7 percent of the value of all arms deliveries worldwide, with a monetary value of nearly US$17bn; the five permanent members of the United Nations Security Council accounted for 90 percent of those deliveries. Meanwhile, across these regions:

-more than a billion people struggled to survive on less than a dollar a day;

-one child in five did not complete primary school;

-more than 14 million children lost one or both parents to AIDS in 2001

-nearly 800 million people suffered from chronic hunger;

-half a million women died in pregnancy or childbirth."

(From Guns or Growth, Control Arms Campaign, June 2004)

Over the ten years the Third World has demonstrated some of the greatest increases in armaments spending. In accounting for this increase, strife in the Far Est, Middle East, Central America and parts of Africa comes immediately to mind, but also unease over boundaries, the prestige value of armed forces, meddling by the great powers are further reasons accounting for an estimated increase of 70 percent in the armed forces of the developing world during this period.

It is tragic that countries already grossly in debt deem it essential to continue to give priority to the buying of arms. All wars since the Second World War have been fought in the Third World, where more than ten million people have been killed. The fact that the military control so many Third World regimes is a contributory factor in excessive military spending and may well be a danger to peace.

During the past decade almost three-quarters of the global arms

"Recent Western conflicts against the Middle East after the end of the Cold War have been part of a new perpetual war. Former U.S. President George H.W. Bush launched attacks on Iraq, Sudan, and Afghanistan to distract the population from his domestic political problems."

— *Robert Fisk, Veteran British journalist*

trade consisted of Third World imports from the industrialised countries. The five permanent members of the UN Security Council, the US, Russia, France, China, and the UK, were also the five leading suppliers of conventional arms to developing countries between 1996 and 2003. And UN Security Council is charged with the maintenance of international peace and security. Foxes are incharge of the chickens.

There is a very nice story. One rat, he was troubled with cat. So he came to a saintly person: "My dear sir, I am very much troubled." "What is the difficulty?" The rat said, "The cat always chases. So I'm not in peace of mind." "Then what do you want?" "Please make me a cat." "All right, you become a cat." After few days, the same cat again came to the saintly person, says, "My dear sir, I am again in trouble." "What is that?" "The dogs are chasing me." "Then what do you want?" "Make me a dog." "All right, you become a dog." Then after few days, again he comes. He says, "I am again in trouble, sir." "What is that?" "The foxes are chasing me." "Then what do you want?" "To become a fox." "All right, you become a fox." Then again he comes. He says, "Oh, tigers are chasing me." "Then what do you want?" "I want to become a tiger." "All right, you become a tiger." And when he became a tiger, he began to stare his eyes on the saintly person: "I shall eat you." "Oh, you shall eat me? I have made you tiger, and you want to eat me?" "Yes, I shall eat you." Oh, then he cursed him, "Again you become a rat." So he became a rat.

So our human civilization is going to be like that. The other day I was reading in your -- what is called? -- World Almanac. In the next hundred years people will live underground like rats. So our scientific advancement has created this atomic bomb to kill man, and it will be used. And we have to go underground to become again rat. From tiger, again rat. That is going to be. That is nature's law. Daivi hy esa gunamayi mama maya duratyaya [Bg. 7.14]. If you defy the laws of your state and you are put into difficulty, similarly if you continue to defy the authority, the supremacy of the Supreme Lord, Personality of Godhead, then the same result: again you become rat. As soon as there is atomic bomb, everything, all civilization on the surface of the globe will be finished. -Prabhupada (Lecture to College Students -- Seattle, October 20, 1968)

Section-II

Economics

Simple & Natural

With A Human Face

"Innocent men, women, they are kept in that factory simply for livelihood. A little work will provide their needs. Nature has given so much facility. They can grow a little food anywhere. The cows are there in the pasturing ground. Take milk and live peacefully. Why you open factories?"
— *Srila Prabhupada (New Vrindavan, June 26, 1976)*

23.

Need For

Total Rethinking On Economic Front

I f humanity and the planet have to survive, then we have to replace the western economic model. Its a fossil fuel based, car-centred, energy inefficient model and promotes over exploitation of natural resources, encourages a throwaway society, creates social injustice and is not viable any longer.

And we have to do it quickly before the geopolitics of oil, grain, and raw material scarcity lead to political conflict and disruption of the social order on which economic progress depends.

The sooner we recognize that our existing economic model cannot sustain economic progress, the better it will be for the entire world. The claims on the earth by the existing model at current consumption levels are such that we are fast depleting the energy and mineral resources on which our modern industrial economy depends. We are also consuming beyond the sustainable yield of the earth's natural systems. As we overcut, overplow, overpump, overgraze, and overfish, we are consuming not only the interest from our natural endowment, we are devouring the endowment itself. In ecology, as in economics, this leads to bankruptcy.

Evidence of this bankruptcy is seen in the economic tremors being felt on either side of the Atlantic.

An Individual Isolated Approach That Ignores The Larger Perspective

Environmental degradation is the most obvious and dangerous consequence to our industrialized, specialized approach to solving problems. Environmental problems have become so pressing that people are now beginning to see how foolish it is to place their faith in individual, isolated disciplines that ignore the larger perspective. They are starting to look at human activities on a broader scale, to see the repercussions their actions have on personal lives, society, and the environment.

From a holistic perspective, economics cannot be separated from other branches of knowledge. Economics is rather one component of a concerted effort to remedy the problems of humanity; and an economics which works for people and the planet would not be so much a self-contained science, but one of a number of interdependent disciplines working in concert toward the common goal of social, individual and environmental well-being.

Just like a diseased person. By controlling... By controlling according to the prescription of the doctor, by controlling himself he becomes reduced in the sufferings of the disease. The fever diminishes from 105 degrees to 102, then 100, then 99, then 98 — he is cured. Similarly, we have to reduce the temperature. We haven't got to increase the temperature. We are just like in the matter of increasing our temperature. We are thinking that by increasing the temperature we shall be happy. We do not know that by increasing temperature we shall never be happy. We have to decrease the temperature. There is a very nice story. Perhaps I have many times told you, that there was a householder, a very rich man. His wife was sick and the maidservant was also sick. So the gentleman called for a doctor, and the doctor treated both the patients, and the doctor said that "Your wife has got 98 temperature, nothing serious. But your maidservant, she has got 104 temperature, so she should be taken care of." Now, the housewife, she became angry. She told the doctor, "Oh, I am the head of the family. I have got only 98 temperature? And my maidservant has got 104? So you are not a doctor!" So that is going on. From 104 we want to increase. 107 degrees and death will come. So the modern civilization is increasing the temperature. So we have come to the point of 107 degree-atom bomb. So we are prepared for killing ourselves. So this degree, this increasing of temperature of material enjoyment will never make us happy.
— Srila Prabhupada (Lecture, Bhagavad-gita, New York, August 31, 1966)

Western academic disciplines and conceptual structures have reached a point which many feel to be a dead end, or if not, at least a turning point demanding new paradigms of thought and methodology. This has led many economists to rethink their isolated, specialized approach. The serious environmental repercussions of rampant consumerism have compelled economists to develop more ecological awareness. Some even propose that all new students of economics incorporate basic ecology into their curriculum.

Unfortunately, as it stands, economics is grossly out of touch with the whole stream of causes and conditions that constitute reality. Economics, and indeed all the social sciences, are, after all, based on man-made or artificial truths.

Our present economics is in gross disharmony with the basic principles of life, nature and universe.

"Darkness of the present age is not due to a lack of material advancement, but that we have lost the clue to our spiritual advancement, which is the prime necessity of human life, the criterion of the highest type of human civilization. Throwing of bombs from airplanes is no advancement of civilization from the primitive, uncivilized practice of dropping big stones on enemies' heads from the tops of hills. . . "

— Srila Prabhupada (Lecture, February 1936, Bombay)

24.

Economics In Harmony

With The Web of Life

Human race does not exist in isolation on this planet but its a minuscule link in a complex web of life. Human survival depends on the survival of life on this planet. The delicate web of life can not be disturbed without endangering the human survival itself. There are millions of species and trillions and quadrillions of other life forms. Fate of all these creatures is intimately connected with that of humanity. Its arrogance and ignorance to think that we can survive in isolation. We, like all other life forms, are products of our environment. Destroying our environment is like cutting off the branch we sit on.

Our present economics is anti-life. Our direct and indirect destruction of life has reached mammoth proportions. In the name of food, we kill over 60 billion animals and birds every year and in the name of economic development, we destroy forests and other species. In fact, It is estimated that a minimum of 54,000 species are becoming extinct each year, about 6 an hour, thanks to our 'development' efforts.

Even though the majority of mankind is happily entrenched in the electronic age and mostly prefers to live in a concrete jungle, the mysterious link between humans and other life forms continues to hold true. Most of our contact with other life forms these days is limited to the fleeting glimpse of a bird overhead, the scurry of a squirrel or chipmunk across our paths, or the companionship of a pet. Yet the role of these life forms in history is of such great importance that we would not be where we are today without them.

Every traditional society which flourished in the annals of history had their animals and were identified with them. You can not think of Native Americans without picturizing their buffalo herds. These buffaloes roaming the great plains shaped their lives and values. In the case of Laplanders, it was their reindeer and in the case of New England whaling villagers, it was the giant whale. Life of Tibetans revolved around their yaks and camel has been the mainstay of Middle East Asian life. For the people of India and Africa, their survival lay in the humble cow.

In each case, without a particular animal the culture of the people would be entirely different. Because of relations to that animal, whether by herding, shooting, or sailing after it, the society encourages attributes such as toughness, bravery, gentleness, or respect for nature.

Animals that did coexist with humans bore a hefty portion of the burden of transporting mankind toward civilization. One thing we do know is that the role of animals in history was crucial and their impact on our future is just as important. While we are spending billions to find life on Mars, animals on earth are going extinct right under our noses.

Any one with an intact brain would admit the obvious and commonplace fact that animals play a conspicuous part in the life of man. Animals affect everyone's life, whether you're an animal-lover, animal-hater, animal-eater or animal-saver.

Every traditional economy was based on its animals and land. That way, the human civilization survived for thousands of years. But in just last one hundred years, everything has been topsy turvied. Survival of humanity and planet itself has come into question. Some one rightly put it, "In the end, cockroaches would prove to be more intelligent than humans if humans destroy themselves. Intelligence is really a survival skill for the entire species and that which survives proves intelligent on a species level."

25.

Life With Animals

Living on Nature's Incomes

Every living being sustains life on the bounties offered by mother nature. The creator is the father and nature is the mother. Mother nature provides for all the necessities of all living beings and in this way every living being can live peacefully in this material world. The human beings, not satisfied with her generous gifts, are devouring the mother nature herself. Its like a child, not satisfied with the mother's milk, want to devour the mother herself.

We, as a society, have come to living off the nature's capital, being dissatisfied with its incomes. In economics, its called bad business. A business enterprise has to survive on its incomes and not on its capital. Capital depletion leads to bankruptcy. In human society, this is leading to our not only ecological but moral, social and economic bankruptcy as well.

At the dawn of the industrial age, we took this wrong turn. We started gorging upon resources that took nature millions of years to create and which were saved up by nature according to its own plan of functioning. Humanity has been squandering these assets at a quickening pace. In fact, we have treated many of these assets as if they had no value.

To check this suicidal drift, we need to seek the animals' cooperation once again. Living with our animals is living in harmony with life, nature and universe. This is the way the life has been for thousands of years or for as long as one can remember.

Living in harmony and cooperation with our animal friends and with our natural world is the ultimate economic security, ultimate survival strategy.

UN biodiversity chief, Ahmed Djoghlaf says nations risk economic collapse and loss of culture if they do not protect the natural world He rightly feels that what we are seeing today is a total disaster as we lose biodiversity at an unprecedented rate. If current levels of destruction go on we will reach a tipping point very soon. The future of the planet now depends on remedial measures taken very soon.

Our callous approach to life and nature is threatening the fundamentals of life itself.

According to the UN Environment Programme, the Earth is in the midst of a mass extinction of life. Scientists estimate that 150-200 species of plant, insect, bird and mammal become extinct every 24 hours. This is nearly 1,000 times the "natural" or "background" rate. Around 15% of mammal species and 11% of bird species are classified as threatened with extinction. UN is urging the  governments to invest in nature. If they do not, they will pay very heavily later. They will be out of business if they miss the green train.

Mounting losses of ecosystems, species and genetic biodiversity is now threatening all life. In immediate danger are the two billion people who live in developing world and whose livelihood depends on their natural resources.

The loss of biodiversity is compounding poverty. By destroying our nature, we are increasing poverty and insecurity. Biodiversity is fundamental to social life, education and aesthetics. It's a human right to live in a healthy environment. Climate change cannot be solved without action on biodiversity, and vice versa.

Because of no contact with the animal world, children are losing contact with nature as they move to a more virtual world. Children today have no clue about nature. Most children in developed countries do not see a live cow or a live horse or an apple tree. How can they protect nature if they do not know it?

Nature has her own way; she better understands her own affairs than we. We have one planet to live on and all our needs have to be satisfied with whatever is in here. We can not import a thing from other planets for our survival, no matter how much we advertise our dubious moon missions. Outcome of such missions is few worthless rocks and sheer wastage of taxpayers' money.

This senseless exploitation of resources can not go on forever. This cradle to grave economics in which we turn every natural resource into a toxic waste is inherently self-destructive. In nature, there is no such thing as waste. So called waste generated by one living being is effectively utilized by another and so on until nothing is left over. This is called the cycle of life. But today our linear system of living which is immensely destructive has replaced this natural cyclical system.

This is where our animals come into picture. Living with animals and natural gifts of land is living on nature's income.

Primitive means very, very old. So whether in the days gone by, people were actually happy or now they are happy?

Even if you say "primitive," the primitive life is very nice. Primitive life means simple life. Keeping pace with the nature's law. It is very nice. Primitive life ... It gives you anxiety-free life, and therefore, even if you take it as primitive, the saintly persons, sages, they used to live long, long years, and their brain was so sharp, because they were taking natural food, fruits, grains, and milk that helps to develop human brain for understanding subtle subject matter. So even Vyasadeva... You have seen the picture of Vyasadeva. He's writing books just near a cottage only. But he's writing. Nobody can create such literature. But he was leading very simple life, in a cottage. Even, say, 2,000 years ago or little more, there was Canakya Pandita. Canakya Pandita, he was a brahmana, but great politician. His politics are studied even now in M.A. class. And because he was a great politician, diplomat, under his name in our India, in New Delhi, the capital, there is a neighborhood which is called Canakya Puri, and all the foreign embassies are there. Your American embassy is also there.

— *Srila Prabhupada*

(Lecture, Srimad-Bhagavatam 2.3.24, Los Angeles, June 22, 1972)

An agriculture and animals based economy is the only model which will stand the test of time. Its just a question of few years before this colossal industrial complex comes down crashing. The cracks are already quite visible and it is upto us to open our eyes.

26.
Role of Animals
In The Upcoming Low-Energy Future

Before the onset of industrialism, animals were omnipresent in people's everyday life. They had enormous importance for medieval agriculture, trade and were an integral part of day-to-day life. People's lives revolved around their animals. Services of animals were used for every conceivable human requirement like - economic development, food production, agriculture, health care, fuel, transport, religious rites, art, culture, recreation, sports, companionship, emotional support, social status, defense, clothing, cottage industry and balancing nature and ecosystems. Thus animals had an all pervasive influence on human cultural patterns and social organizations.

Discovery of fossil fuels and subsequent industrial revolution changed all that. Role of animals in services like transport and traction was increasingly replaced with machines. The period saw significant changes in scientific and philosophical approaches to animals. In the industrialized urban setting, the animals' main role came to garnish our dinner plates.

But this 200 years old techno-industrial complex has run into difficulties. It is entering a decisive phase now as the resources run scarce to satisfy its ravenous appetite. Human society, living an industrialized life, has used up resources which took nature millions of years to build up. How long our earth and environment can support this reckless living is a question now.

On many fronts, the crumbling of this colossal industrial setup is becoming apparent. One on the forefront is peak oil or upcoming oil shortage. Oil is the lifeblood of modern civilization and choke off the oil and it quickly seizes.

With no viable alternatives in sight, human society is facing today a great crisis of unprecedented scale. All the previous calamities were local in nature. Oil crisis would be a global disaster because the world today shares a common fate, thanks to interdependence and interconnectivity. Earlier we suffered in isolation and now we go down, all together. There are food riots in Africa when America decides to produce bio-fuels. When there are skirmishes in Nigeria, a government is toppled on other side of the globe.

Chevron, a major oil company in the world, its homepage (WillYouJoinUs) reads:

"Energy will be one of the defining issues of the century. One thing is clear: the era of easy oil is over. So let the discussion begin. How will we meet the energy needs of the entire world in this century and beyond?"

Discovery of fossil fuels ushered in an era of industrial revolution two centuries years ago. This in turn gave birth to many isms like capitalism, communism, socialism, Darwinism etc.

This century will see the dawn of an era in which fossil fuels begin to deplete. This will signal the death of many 'isms' that cropped up with the discovery of fossil fuels. Armed with the enormous power of fossil fuels, man mistook himself to be the God and gradually alienated himself with the nature and his Creator. But this arrogance is all set to end sometime soon.

Peak Oil : A Silent Tsunami Approaching Humanity

Oil is a non-renewable resource. We have always known that yet the world has been behaving as if oil is in endless supply. And even underdeveloped nations who have lived in a biodiversity and biomass energy economy are rushing into oil addiction precisely when the global oil supply is running low and prices are running high.

Peak oil means the end of cheap oil, and an end to economies organized around the increasing availability of cheap oil. As first expressed in Hubbert peak theory, peak oil is the point or timeframe at which the maximum global petroleum production rate is reached. After this timeframe, the rate of production will by definition enter terminal decline. According to the Hubbert model, production will follow a roughly symmetrical bell-shaped curve.

The Association for the Study of Peak Oil (ASPO), an umbrella organization of oil experts, mainly geologists who helped find oil fields are now warning us that there are only a trillion barrels or less of oil left, and the supply will peak any time now. Beyond "peak oil", there will be an overall decline in production and an increase in oil prices.

The peak is the top of the curve, the halfway point of the world's all-time total endowment, meaning half the world's oil will be left. That seems like a lot of oil, and it is, but there's a big catch: It's the half that is much more difficult to extract, far more costly to get, of much poorer quality and located mostly in places which are politically instable. A substantial amount of it will never be extracted.

That global oil output will eventually reach a peak and then decline is no longer a matter of debate; all major energy organizations have now embraced this view. What remains open for argument is precisely when this moment will arrive. Whatever the timing of this momentous event, it is apparent that the world faces a profound shift in the global availability of energy, as we move from a situation of relative abundance to one of relative scarcity.

The exact moment of peak oil's arrival is not as important as the fact that world oil output will almost certainly fall short of global demand, given the fossil-fuel voraciousness of the older industrialized nations, especially the United States, and soaring demand from China, India, and other rapidly growing countries. The U.S. Department of Energy (DoE) projects global oil demand to grow by 35% between 2004 and 2025 -- from 82 million to 111 million barrels per day.

Much of the world's easy-to-acquire petroleum has already been extracted and significant portions of what remains can only be found in places that present significant drilling challenges like the hurricane-prone Gulf of Mexico or the iceberg-infested waters of the North Atlantic - or in perennially conflict-ridden and sabotage-vulnerable areas of Africa, Central Asia, and the Middle East.

This is a warning call to rethink how we plan our cities and what we think constitutes our economy. Our economy must be structured to adapt to this new reality. In the low energy future, local will be everything.

As the realities of climate change and peak oil are realized globally it is important to develop approaches that will help each of us transition to a lower energy existence.

Disillusionment With Nuclear Energy
A Dangerous Journey From Hiroshima To Fukushima

The Nuclear Age began in July 1945 when the US tested their first nuclear bomb near Alamogordo, New Mexico. A few years later, in 1953, President Eisenhower launched his "Atoms for Peace" Programme at the UN amid a wave of unbridled atomic optimism.

But as we know there is nothing "peaceful" about all things nuclear. More than half a century after Eisenhower's speech the planet is left with the legacy of nuclear waste.

No nation on Earth has yet met the engineering challenge of safely storing waste that will emit dangerous levels of radioactivity for thousands of years. Nuclear power is an unacceptable risk to the environment and to humanity. The only solution is to halt the expansion of all nuclear power, and for the shutdown of existing plants.

We need an energy system that can fight climate change, based on renewable energy and energy efficiency. Nuclear power already delivers less energy globally than renewable energy, and the share will continue to decrease in the coming years.

Things are moving slowly in the right direction. In November 2000

"Nuclear power plants are, next to nuclear warheads themselves, the most dangerous devices that man has ever created. Their construction and proliferation is the most irresponsible, in fact the most criminal act ever to have taken place on this planet."
— *Patrick Moore, Assault on Future Generations, 1976*

the world recognised nuclear power as a dirty, dangerous and unnecessary technology by refusing to give it greenhouse gas credits during the UN climate change talks in The Hague. Nuclear power was dealt a further blow when a UN sustainable development conference refused to label nuclear a sustainable technology in April 2001.

The risks from nuclear energy are real, inherent and long-lasting.

Animal Power

Before 200 years, most energy was renewable – animal and human muscle, wood, some wind and water power.

As we saw in foregoing paragraphs, the world economy's addiction to oil, gas, and coal is unsustainable. All these fuels were formed millions of year ago and once used up cannot be replaced. But before industrial revolution, practically all the energy used was renewable.

For millennia animals have been harnessed to pull carts, carry loads, transport people, haul water, trash harvests, plough, puddle and weed crop fields etc. *Even today, more than half the world's population depends on animal power* for much of its energy. Draught animals operate on more than 50% of the planet's cultivated areas. In the mid 1990s work by draught animals was estimated to be equivalent to a fossil fuel replacement value of US$ 6 billion. Estimates of the number of animals used for power applications range from 300 million upwards. Oxen are the most frequently used animals and ploughing is the most common function. Almost all species of domestic quadruped are used, however, in a variety of agricultural and transport roles. In agriculture positive effects are seen to be higher crop output, better returns to labour, increased cash income and improved food security.

Despite motorization on all fronts the use of animals is still often more economic than the use of machinery and vehicles, especially in small scale agriculture and in remote areas. Animals are produced and maintained locally and don't require the infrastructure needed for motorization. Where the value of machinery needs to be depreciated over time, that of animals can appreciate because of growth.

Ox power represents a sustainable and renewable resource of energy. In terms of agriculture, ox power creates a lighter footprint on the earth than a tractor, which tends to compact the soil. Also in terms of the environment, it takes far less resources to produce a team of oxen than a tractor. How many mining operations and how many factories does it require to produce even one tractor? How many drilling and refining operations does it take to fuel it? The "factory" that produces an ox is a cow. For "fuel" the oxen can eat grass and grain which they themselves produce.

And, we should not underestimate the level of benefit that oxen can provide. Without any exception, practically every materially advanced civilization before the crusades – including China, India, the Middle East, North Africa and Europe – relied on oxen to be the engine for agriculture, local transport, grinding grains and even building. Many of the great projects of ancient times were all accomplished without the incredible level of pollution it would take to recreate such structures today.

The tractor is a real sore point in agriculture. Tractors are expensive to operate. This expense partly explains why 30,000 to 50,000 small farms collapse every year in US. But ox power, though slower, is far more efficient.

For small farms, oxen do better than tractors. They require no gasoline, cost far less than tractors to maintain, provide free fertilizer, preserve precious topsoil, and don't foul the atmosphere with carbon monoxide. Bovine waste, when mixed in the traditional way with straw, is the world's best fertilizer. And when the animal dies, its skin can be processed into leather.

Turning to Gandhi for inspiration, we find that a key requirement for building peace is to provide full employment by emphasizing localized production for localized markets. Gandhi stressed that everything which

"Petrol is required for long-distance transport, but if you are localized, there is no question of such transport. You don't require petrol.... The oxen will solve the problem of transport."
—Srila Prabhupada (Morning Walk, May 27, 1974, Rome)

can be produced locally should be, even if the local economy is less efficient at its production. Since time immemorial, human cultures have lived with and protected cows. Cows have provided many essential services to humanity for very little maintenance. They're inseparably part of God's efficient system for human civilization. Today people employ them in agriculture in India and many other so-called developing countries.

Dr. Vandana Shiva, an ecologist, comments on India's recent cattle policy while calling it a policy of ecocide of indigenous cattle breeds and a policy of genocide for India's small farmers: "The traditional approach to livestock is based on diversity, decentralisation, sustainability and equity. Our cattle are not just milk machines or meat machines. They are sentient beings who serve human communities through their multidimensional role in agriculture."

"On the other hand," continues Shiva, "externally driven projects, programmes and policies emerging from industrial societies treat cattle as one-dimensional machines which are maintained with capital intensive and environmentally intensive inputs and which provide a single output - either milk or meat. Polices based on this approach are characterised by monocultures, concentration and centralisation, non-sustainability and inequality."

Thus, whether we like it or not, when fossil fuels bid us good bye, world will have to revert back to more sustainable options for fulfilling its energy requirements.

27.

A New Kind of Dairy Product : Cow Power

Shift From Natural Gas To A Very Natural Gas

In the last chapter we heard the story of fossil fuels and heard that this story may not have a very happy ending. In this chapter we will examine biomass as an alternative energy source.

To begin with, lets take the example of a developing economy like India. In 1980, India's oil import bill was $6.6 billion and it shot up to a whopping $101.7 in 2010.

With close to 70% of its oil requirements imported from more than 8 countries, India is a net importer of oil. By 2020, around 92% of India's total oil demand has to be met by imports. For a country which is home to the highest number of malnourished children in the world, this is a lot of money. India's oil bill takes priority over health care, education and agriculture. With over one hundred farmers committing suicide each day, India Inc's first priority is its oil bill. With instable global prices and rapidly rising domestic demand, India today stands at the cross roads, without a clue.

But a prominent Indian Industrialist, Arun Firodia, Chairman of Kinetic Group offers a solution to this predicament in his article "Cows Are Forever: Methane Gas the Answer to Oil Imports", published in Times of India on December 8, 2004.

"(Former) US president George W Bush recently made a fervent appeal to the developed world to take to methane farming. He rightly said methane farming would counter the skyrocketing prices of crude oil and emerge as an alternative to fossil fuels whose stocks may be depleted in the next 30-40 years. Methane farming is nothing but generation of biogas from starch or organic waste such as cowdung. A developing country like India should take up methane farming, in view of our rapidly growing energy requirements."

"We have the world's largest livestock population of 250 million, which produces close to 125 million tonnes of cowdung. Using this we can produce enough methane gas to entirely replace LPG and kerosene in cooking, and substitute petrol in transportation. Methane gas can also generate enough electricity to meet all requirements, at least in rural

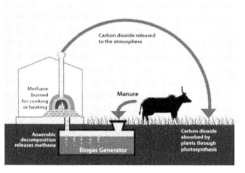

areas. The by-product can serve as excellent organic manure, substituting chemical fertilisers which require LNG as feedstock."

"The gobar gas research station in Uttar Pradesh has established that one cow gives enough cowdung in a year to produce methane gas equivalent to 225 litres of petrol in energy terms. The calorific value table would show that one kg of methane gas is more or less equal in energy content to one kg of petrol, LPG, kerosene or diesel."

"LPG is generally used for cooking in urban areas while kerosene is the preferred fuel in rural India. A 15 kg LPG cylinder lasts about two months for a family of six. This works out to 15 kg of LPG per capita per year. The same holds true for kerosene. The entire LPG and kerosene requirements of our 100 crore population can be met by methane gas cylinders, produced from the cowdung of 75 million cows."

"Just like CNG, methane gas can be used to run automobile engines in place of petrol. Our petrol consumption last year (2003-04) was

"What we can say without a shadow of doubt is petroleum man will be just about extinct by the end of this century. That poses the thorny difficult question: Will Homo sapiens be so wise as his name implies and figure out a way to live without oil which is the bloodstream of virtually everything?"
— *Dr Colin Campbell*

eight million tonnes. On the assumption that one cow produces methane gas equivalent to 225 litres of petrol, we will need about 40 million cows to produce an energy equivalent to eight million tonnes of petrol. A generator needs 200 gm of petrol to produce one kilowatt/hour (kwH) of electrical energy. The per capita electrical energy consumption in rural area is 112 kwH per annum. Our rural population being 74 crore, we will need another 85 million cows to meet the electrical energy needs of rural areas. This comes to a total of 200 million livestock to satisfy our energy requirements."

"Obtaining methane gas from cowdung is simple enough. It consists of an airtight tank filled with raw organic waste like cowdung. The anaerobic decay of this matter generates gobar gas. An agitator quickens the process. The gas is collected in an inverted  drum. This gas has 68 per cent methane and 31 per cent carbon dioxide. It is passed through lime water to remove the carbon dioxide and over iron fillings to remove HoS. It then becomes enriched with methane."

"The gobar gas plants are available in various sizes, from three cubic meters to 270 cubic meters, costing between Rs 20,000 and Rs 100,000. A compressor can extract and compress this methane gas into portable cylinders. These methane gas cylinders can then be used for cooking, or in automobiles and two wheelers. As much as 50 per cent of the cowdung slurry is available as leftover in the gobar gas plant, which then can be used to produce organic manure rich in nitrogen and phosphorus. The cowdung of 200 million cows can produce 50 million tonnes of manure, which can be used for two rotations in a year to take care of the fertiliser needs of the entire 143 million hectares in the country. This will completely offset the need to import LNG, used as feedstock in fertiliser plants."

"If every village (of which we have 6.27 lakh) has 50 farmer families who maintain just two bullocks and four cows each, the cowdung of these animals can produce enough methane gas to take care of country's entire energy needs, now being met by LPG, kerosene, petrol and LNG. Besides, this livestock can provide rural electricity as well. Why should we import oil from the Gulf or gas in a pipeline via a hostile Pakistan, when we can manage from our resources?" ©Times of India Group.

This article, published in India's most prominent daily, is not an utopian idea or an impractical dream. Its happening in many parts of the world. The dairies world over are now producing power to cut costs and even marketing it outside. Among the thousands of examples, Liaoning Huishan Cow Farm in China is one.

This farm has the world's largest waste-to-energy biogas project based on cow manure – from 250,000 cows – and is producing 38,000 MWh annually and reducing CO_2 emissions by 180,000 tons per year.

Helping to alleviate China's energy shortage, Jenbacher biogas engines are powering the world's largest biogas project based on cow manure. The manure from the 250,000 cows at the farm, located in Shenyang, China, is being converted into biogas and is producing 38,000 MWh a year through four GE Jenbacher gas engines. The energy generated is being sold to the state grid in China.

One of the features of the project is the utilization of fuel circulation. In addition to the use of biogas for power generation, the liquid (residual from biogas production) is being used to nourish the grass in the pasture, and the solid waste is being sold as organic fertilizer, thus the surrounding land is becoming a base for organic agriculture.

Its serving China's national economic and environmental development goals. Mr. Xu Guangyi, vice president of Liaoning Huishan Cow Farm says, "The disposal and treatment of biological waste represents a major challenge for the waste industry. But we are meeting this challenge by maximizing the use of an economical energy supply - cow manure."

Biogas offers customers several advantages. It provides an alternative disposal of dung, liquid manure and biowaste, while simultaneously harnessing them as an energy source, a substitute for conventional fuels. It also has the high potential for reduction in greenhouse gases and is highly efficient for combined on-site power and heat generation. In addition, the remaining substrate from the digester can be used as high-quality, agricultural fertilizer, characterized by neutralizing the acid effect with a higher ph-value, keeping nutrients retained and nearly odorless.

Like the Huishan gas energy project, other countries in the world are harnessing their own diverse renewable and alternative resources to create cleaner sources of energy.

The Big question: Can Cow Dung Energy Solve Global Energy Woes?

This question could fairly go unanswered at this point of time just because it does not need an explanation. Even a fifth grader today, could blindly recognize the need to shift to better, cleaner and safer sources of energy. Oil has already played its menacing role under the disguise of the greatest source of energy. Renewable energy should be a compulsion instead of being a point of discussion now.

The cows which are generally used for milk, transportation and farming are now found to be a greatest asset because of their dung which is potentially a new break through to supply the future energy demands of the world.

A Booming Energy Sector

Cow dung energy is a booming renewable energy sector. It also has a whopping annual growth of 25-30%. The electrical energy produced from cow dung is slowly becoming an integral part of the gigantic global energy market. This sector received an investment of around $100bn in the year 2006. The Biogas Support Program (BSP) developed in Nepal has created a very comfortable financial situation for the Nepalese and it has also proved to be beneficial for both the industrial world as well as the atmosphere.

This model project recently won several national and international accolades including the prestigious Ashden Award for Sustainable Energy and the project is also being incorporated into several Asian and African nations. And if that was not enough, the researchers are also developing a data center completely powered by energy generated from cow dung. We may soon be expecting computers powered by cow dung.

A bio-gas powered train has been running in Sweden from 2005.

T-systems a German based IT company has started using bio-gas based fuel cells to keep its servers cool and is able to cut energy costs considerably.

In the suburbs of Seattle, a fuel cell, located at the South Treatment Plant in Renton, WA, consumes about 154,000 cubic feet of biogas a day to produce up to 1 MW of electricity. That's enough to power 1,000 households, but right now it's being used instead to help operate the plant.

Kompogas' Biogas facility in Otelfingen is a large scale composting facility where over 10,000 tons of material per year is turned into nearly 1.3 million liters of biogas.

Bio gas run vehicles have a range of 250-400kms. Like Volvo, worldwide many vehicles are being manufactured that run on biogas. Biogas can share distribution facilities with CNG and is currently used as fuel in more than four million vehicles.

Moo-ve Over Wind And Solar Energy - Cow Dung Is Here!

For ages, cow dung traditionally has been used as manure in the fields, but it is also a source of viable energy- bio gas, which can reduce greenhouse emissions significantly. Being used in various developing countries for over three decades now, biomass has a lot of potential to reduce carbon footprint. By capturing and storing CO_2 from biogas into the ground, the biogas becomes carbon negative and scrubs our past CO_2 emissions out of the atmosphere.

Europe is coming in a big way to use Biogas, where it is being developed on a large scale for the production of fuels for stationary power generation (to be used in natural gas plants or in fuel cells) as well as for the transport sector. It is being fed into the natural gas grid  (attracting subsidies) or in dedicated pipelines supplying cities. Some European countries have thousands of farm-based digesters and are producing significant quantities of biogas. Carbon Finance, put together by World Bank for United Nation's Clean development fund to allow rich developed nations which are not adhering to the Kyoto Protocol, to buy emissions that poor countries prevent through conserving forests or promoting renewable energy. Nepal's biogas programme has overtaken China and India, per capita wise. Called BSP (bio-gas support program) each bio gas plant is said to prohibit the entry of about 4.6 tonnes of green house gases into the atmosphere every year. This is a model bio-gas project developed in rural Nepal. This bio-gas plant is predicted to not only save the CO_2 emission by a huge percentage, its by-product, i.e., the waste from the digester can be used as compost.

Rich countries are buying this 'saved' greenhouse gas worth many millions for the illegal emissions they produce.

How Is Biogas made?

Its fairly simple. All they have to do is to collect the manure from cows, mix it with water and leaves it to ferment in a large concrete tank  or pit. The gas produced is collected in a simple storage tank, from where it is piped into the house to use. Biogas is perhaps the cheapest way to convert waste into energy. The initial cost is of about $100-300, for setting up a biodigester, grants for which are available in most of the countries. The concept of biogas is more suited to systems where waste is treated near the source, there by reducing transport and initial costs.

There are three types of digesters that have been developed so far, namely: 1. Fixed dome plant, which was developed in china, 2. Floating drum plant, which is more widely used in India with a variant cover plastic biogas plant, and 3. Plug-flow balloon plant or a plant which is widely used in Taiwan, Ethiopia, Colombia, Vietnam and Cambodia.

Principal parts of bio-gas digester are: 1. container vessel animal manure, 2. digester, 3. slurry tanks, 4. gas reservoir, 5. gas pipe exit, 6. slurry pipe exit, 7. intake of cattle dung.

A revolution In The Third World

A few decades ago, a silent revolution took place in many developing countries of the world. Rural India, Sri Lanka, China, Nepal, Malaysia, Vietnam, Turkey; third world countries were facing problems with growing prices of fossil fuels and dependence on forests was affecting the ecology. Most of the economy of these countries is still largely dependant on agriculture. These countries have large cattle herds, producing tones of manure. Biogas, a choice which relieved poor farmers from the burden of managing tones of dung, also provided rich manure for their

fields, from its residue. It came as a boon. How it has benefited poor farmers of the Third World- In rural India, where agricultural residues are huge and dung from India's 300 million cattle a major problem, bio gas has become a source of energy to more than 3 million homes. Areas which were deprived of any are now self sufficient; from cooking, doing laundry to lighting, all without burning even a single piece of wood; it has even provided permanent jobs for the unemployed. -The gas has cleanly replaced firewood, dung, agricultural residues, petrol, diesel and electricity, depending on the nature of the task, and local supply conditions and constraints. There is very little waste from it therefore making it environmentally viable. - A smoke and ash free kitchen it has become boon for the women as it saves the time wasted in collecting fire wood and has reduced the chances of chronic respiratory diseases. Far less energy is required in making biogas than tree felling. Now the forests are also getting protected thus allowing the forests to regenerate. The sludge remaining after air free digestion is superior in quality, resulting in better nutrient quality of fruits and vegetables, over the usual organic fertilizer, cow dung. Farmers can sell the produce as organic. Dung is no longer stored at home for cooking food, it feeds the degrader instead. The anaerobic digestion process also destroys pathogens.

Modern Implications of Bio Gas

Biogas became a success in the rural because the raw material required for it is cheap. This flammable gas is mainly used for cooking and heating it is well suited to run mobile engines as well.

A fuel that can be replenished in 2 weeks time, is definitely worth considering over fossil fuels. Rural sector having successfully adopted the technology, it is well suited for urban areas as well where solid waste disposal has become a common problem. Rich countries are following the path shown by developing countries and soon there will more areas explored with in the biogas.

Power House In Every Backyard

The main advantage of using bio-gas as an alternate source for energy is that it decentralizes the energy sources as each house can have its own localized bio-gas module and become self-sufficient in all its energy needs and also rendering freedom from fossil fuels.

The governments of many developed countries are looking forward to take serious steps toward promoting this energy campaign. There are even attempts to build cow farms outside some cities so that even the urban community may also enjoy the fruits of a better fuel for the community, the world and also mother earth.

Advantages of Bio-gas From Cow Dung

Cow dung gas is 55-65% methane, 30-35% carbon dioxide, with some hydrogen, nitrogen and other traces. Its heating value is around 600 B.T.U. per cubic foot. Natural gas consists of around 80 % methane, yielding a B.T.U. value of about 1000.

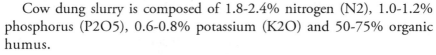

Bio-gas may be improved by filtering it through limewater to remove carbon dioxide, iron filings to absorb corrosive hydrogen sulphide and calcium chloride to extract water vapour after the other two processes.

Cow dung slurry is composed of 1.8-2.4% nitrogen (N2), 1.0-1.2% phosphorus (P2O5), 0.6-0.8% potassium (K2O) and 50-75% organic humus.

About one cubic foot of gas may be generated from one pound of cow manure at around 28°C. This is enough gas to cook a day's meals for 4-6 people in India.

About 1.7 cubic meters of biogas equals one litre of gasoline. The manure produced by one cow in one year can be converted to methane which is the equivalent of over 225 litres of gasoline.

The Only Way To Save Our Forests

All over the Third World, biogas is helping save thousands of hectares of forests every year. For example, in Xinjiang of China, the rural residents have stopped using firewood and turned to methane gas since two years ago. Before this, each family burnt about 500 kilograms of wood from the trees that are used to mitigate desertification. In this area alone, annually 1,70,000 tons of trees and shrubs were burnt for cooking. They don't need to buy firewood anymore, as methane gas is cleaner and more convenient.

Since 2003, the Chinese government has invested about USD 27million in installing methane gas facilities derived from waste management. Since then, deforestation has been reduced to minimum.

In Nepal there are about 124 000 domestic biogas plants. The plants use cow manure to provide biogas (mostly methane) for cooking and lighting. The Project has greatly improved the living conditions there. About 80% of the Nepal farms uses wood, cattle waste and agricultural residues for cooking and kerosene for lighting. Women have to spend hours each day in distant jungles in search of depleting wood supply. Biogas utilization now benefits about one million people (4% of the population of Nepal), and the biogas sector provides about 11,000 permanent jobs in the country.

There are similar success stories from Africa and other parts of the Third World as well.

Home Grown Energy - The Future of Humanity

Hundreds of companies all over the world are now specializing in biogas technologies. In India, one South Indian company, Arjun Energy Corporation, Salem, has developed a mini biogas digester which costs less than USD100. It gives 1 cubic meter of gas which is enough for a family of 5-6, and also gives organic manure around 25kgs per day which is sufficient for 7 acres of land.

And it needs input of cowdung from just 2 cows.

User can recover the cost of the investment in just 3-6 months. Many homes are running generators on biogas, without using a single drop of diesel and saving money on the power bills.

Perpetual And Dependable Source of Power

This is an energy starved world. The economic progress and development has brought us to a spot where we are paralyzed without

"It's been a magnificent success. No problems so far. The system produces more gas than my camp's staff can consume. I'm trying to get them to run it out, and they can't do it."
—*Hotelier Garry Cullen, who uses the Flexi Biogas system at home and at his luxury tented camp in the Mara.*

an organized, perpetual and dependable source of power. But for cheap power, our computers would stop, factories and stores would close, fans, air conditions, TVs, lights and heaters wont work, irrigation pumps would stop and life as we know would come to a grinding halt.

The greatest engineering challenge of the day is to find a good source of power which will be perpetual, dependable, renewable, affordable, and available in adequate quantities and above all environmental friendly. Present sources of power like gas, coal, hydro and nuclear fuels do not fit this description. Of course experiment is going on with solar, wind and tidal source.

Many governments are working on various projects to meet their energy requirements from one of the world's most ancient fuels - the cow dung. The omnipresent and the humble cow's excreta will become increasingly important in coming years. Time has come where the focus would soon shift from high milk yielding cows to high dung yielding cows. Soon, milk might come to be regarded as an extra byproduct.

Its hardly surprising as cow dung is already the mainstay energy source for hundreds of millions of people in the underdeveloped countries.

Cow dung is an excellent fuel and it helps preserve world's fossil fuel reserves. It is odorless and burns without scorching, giving a slow, even heat. A housewife can count on leaving her pots unattended all day or return any time to a preheated griddle for short-order cooking. To replace dung with coal would cost a country like India $21.5 billion per year.

Cow Dung To Heat British Homes

British homes would soon be heated by gas produced from cow manure and sewage slurry, under plans being considered by Centrica, the owner of British Gas.

The company, which has 16 million UK customers, is drawing up plans to build a plant that would use cow manure to produce biomethane that could be injected directly into the national gas network. National Grid has estimated that such biogas could supply 18 per cent of total UK demand for gas — or 18 billion cubic meters of the approximately 100 billion total consumed in Britain every year.

A spokesman for Centrica said that biogas was an "interesting technology." John Baldwin, a biomethane consultant with CNG Services, which is advising Centrica, said that the industry remained "embryonic" in the UK but was well advanced in continental countries. However, he said that the economics of British biomethane production would be transformed in April 2011, when the Government begins a subsidy scheme called the Renewable Heat Incentive.

By the end of this year, the Government is poised to set a premium that will be paid to biomethane producers from 2011, potentially unleashing a flood of investment into the industry.

About 15,000 cars in Sweden use this fuel, which is available in filling stations.

Cars That Run on Cow Power

Race cars have long provided a testing ground for driving technology that we eventually see in passenger cars on the road. To this end, an engineering team in Lancashire, England, is hoping to give cow power a place in mass-produced consumer automobiles by creating a race car that runs on cow manure. Yes, there are hopes that by processing cow waste and using it to fuel cars, it can reduce the impact of fossil fuels that contribute to global warming.

Using cow power to win a rally championship may seem like a tall order, but these engineers are up to the challenge. The process, which has been gaining attention worldwide, uses fermented cow dung and anaerobic digesters to provide natural gas fuel. Rally racing is an intense form of motorsports that pushes car on-and-off road, and racers quickly figure out what does or doesn't work. Oacktec has already developed hybrid-electric motors for Honda, so they plan on using a Honda Civic Hybrid to compete within a year.

Using a hybrid car that runs partially on cow manure may provide an interesting alternative to current gasoline-electric hybrids. The world is watching with interest how cow power performs on the racetrack.

In another experiment, The Vehicle Research Institute of Western Washington University has been turning cow manure into fuel that can power a natural-gas car. Researchers are not shoveling manure straight into the gas tank but pumping the methane - the gas created by the manure - into the car.

They have some hard-working cows at a dairy farm in Lyndon, Washington, to thank for this experiment, which could mean cheaper car fuel for many people. For 21 days, the manure sits in an underground tank and stews. Then, using regular old garden hoses, researchers siphon floating methane out of the holding tank.

Every cow can produce enough manure in a day to make a car go about 15 miles. Unfortunately, there are not enough cows in the United States to power every vehicle. But Vehicle Research Institute researchers say a natural-car powered by methane could be a great solution for certain rural communities.

The price of cow fuel will put some consumers, well, over the moon. The gas is currently being sold at one-fifth the pump price. The secret to cheaper gas lies in cow dung!

Cows May Soon Power Computers!

Cow manure may soon be used as a source of energy to power data centers or Internet in the future.

Hewlett-Packard has released a study called "Design of Farm Waste-Driven Supply Side Infrastructure for Data Centers" that draws attention to biogas energy created from cow dung. The study encourages dairy farmers to rent out land and power to technology companies.

This uses the same process described earlier of transforming cow manure to biofuel called biogas. This gas can be used as natural gas or diesel fuel in generators that produce electricity.

Cow Power - An Ancient Future

Aside from these high profile experiments, cow power is already the lifeline of many countries and more may join the list once the oil supplies peak. Here we see the example of India, the second most populous country in the world.

The world cattle population is close to one billion out of which over 200 million indigenous cows reside in India. This accounts for one-fifth of the world's cattle population. In more recent years, some economists have come to agree that cow is essential to world's economy. Cows are the greatest natural resource. They eat only grass --which grows everywhere--and generates more power than all of the generating plants in developing countries. They also produce fuel, fertilizer, and nutrition in abundance. Many developing countries run on bullock power. In India, some 15 million bullock carts move approximately 15 billion tons of goods across the nation. Newer studies in energetics have shown that bullocks do two-thirds of the work on the average farm in developing countries. Electricity and fossil fuels account for only 10%. Bullocks not only pull heavy loads, but also grind the sugarcane and turn the oil presses. In India itself, converting from bullocks to machinery would cost an estimated $30 billion plus maintenance and replacement costs.

Agricultural is still the mainstay of developing economies like India. Cow breeding and cow preservation are integral to it. 75 per cent of Indians live in villages and derive the greatest benefits from cows and bullocks. Despite the compulsions of modernism, tractors are not suitable for Indian land holdings unlike in the US and UK. In US the land available to each person is around 14 acre; in India it is around 0.70 acre. A tractor consumes diesel, creates pollution, doesn't eat grass nor produces dung for manure. So for Indian conditions ploughing is still ideal. Even Albert Einstein, in a letter to Sir CV Raman, wrote: "Tell the people of India, that if they want to survive and show the world path to survive, then they should forget about tractor and preserve their ancient tradition of ploughing."

India has more than 6,00,000 villages, many which do not have asphalted motorable roads. In hilly regions where even a horse cannot tread, oxen can pull their carts with ease.

Boasting of the largest rail road network of the world, Indian Railways transported 55.7 crore tons of goods in 2004-05. In the same year, the humble ox cart transported 278.5 crore tons. In the same year, trains moved 511.2 crore passengers while ox carts catered to 2044.8 crore passengers.

Most importantly, the carts do not produce air or sound pollution and there are no accidents, even when the drivers dozes off.

28.

Cow And Farming
In A Low-Energy Future

We are eating oil and drinking oil. Oil is at the heart of industrial food production and processing, and long distance food transport. The systems that produce the world's food supply are heavily dependent on fossil fuels. Vast amounts of oil and gas are used as raw materials and energy in the manufacture of fertilisers and pesticides, and as cheap and readily available energy at all stages of food production: from planting, irrigation, feeding and harvesting, through to processing, distribution and packaging. In addition, fossil fuels are essential in the construction and the repair of equipment and infrastructure needed to facilitate this industry, including farm machinery, processing facilities, storage, ships, trucks and roads. The industrial food supply system is one of the biggest consumers of fossil fuels and one of the greatest producers of greenhouse gases.

Food security is increasingly coming under scanner in recent years as the law of diminishing returns sets in agriculture. How long our fields can support chemical inundation and reckless cultivation methods like monocroping.

Year 2007 saw ''great wheat panic" grip the world and year 2008 is witnessing rationing of rice in USA, of all places, and food riots in dozens of countries.

More than oil, its "cheap" oil that is crucial for the survival of modern food industry. Virtually all of the processes in the modern food system are dependent upon this finite resource, which is nearing its depletion phase.

Not only is the contemporary food system inherently unsustainable, increasingly, it is damaging the environment.

Proximity and localisation of food system would be beneficial. Ironically, the food industry is at serious risk from global warming caused by these greenhouse gases, through the disruption of the predictable climactic cycles on which agriculture depends.

Environmental degradation, water shortages, salination, soil erosion, pests, disease and desertification all pose serious threats to our food supply, and are made worse by climate change.

Industrial agriculture and the systems of food supply are also responsible for the erosion of communities throughout the world. This social degradation is compounded by trade rules and policies, by the profit driven mindset of the industry, and by the lack of knowledge of the faults of the current systems and the possibilities of alternatives. But the globalisation and corporate control that seriously threaten society and the stability of our environment are only possible because

cheap energy is used to replace labour and allows the distance between producer and consumer to be extended.

However, this is set to change. Oil output is expected to peak in the next few years and steadily decline thereafter. We have a very poor understanding of how the extreme fluctuations in the availability and cost of both oil and natural gas will affect the global food supply systems, and how they will be able to adapt to the decreasing availability of energy. In the near future, environmental threats will combine with energy scarcity to cause significant food shortages and sharp increases in prices - at the very least. We are about to enter an era where we will have to once again feed the world with limited use of fossil fuels. But do we have enough time, knowledge, money, energy and political power and will to make this massive transformation to our food systems when they are already threatened by significant environmental stresses and increasing corporate control?

Just how energy inefficient the food system is can be seen in the crazy case of the Swedish tomato ketchup. Researchers at the Swedish Institute for Food and Biotechnology analysed the production of tomato ketchup. The study considered the production of inputs to agriculture, tomato cultivation and conversion to tomato paste (in Italy), the processing and packaging of the paste and other ingredients into tomato ketchup in Sweden and the retail and storage of the final product. All this involved more than 52 transport and process stages.

The aseptic bags used to package the tomato paste were produced in the Netherlands and transported to Italy to be filled, placed in steel barrels, and then moved to Sweden. The five layered, red bottles were either produced in the UK or Sweden with materials form Japan, Italy, Belgium, the USA and Denmark. The polypropylene (PP) screw-cap of the bottle and plug, made from low density polyethylene (LDPE), was produced in Denmark and transported to Sweden. Additionally, LDPE shrink-film and corrugated cardboard were used to distribute the final product. Labels, glue and ink were not included in the analysis.

Another example of how much fossil fuel goes into our food is our sandwich:

1. And we look first at the bread: we have to plant the cereal using a diesel tractor – this means ploughing, harrowing, drill the seeds. Then in conventional farming we add a load of chemicals to make it grow, and to protect the crop we add fungicides, herbicides, insecticides, all made from oil. Then extra nutrients in the form of chemical food is given, derived from natural gas. Then the wheat is harvested, and then driven to be processed.

2. If it is not a vegetarian sandwich, then the meat it contains has more fossil fuel in it. Cows and pigs are even more energy hungry in that they are fed on grains.

3. Now the salad – this is either shipped or flown or grown in a heated greenhouse which uses a huge amount of energy. 4. Then is this is all either cooked or cooled or both and driven miles and miles before being assembled into a sandwich.

Basically the sandwich is dripping in oil as a result of the way our food production is today. We will starve if we have no oil refineries. Farming and food production without oil will grind to a halt.

This example demonstrates the extent to which the food system is now dependent on national and international freight transport. However, there are many other steps involved in the production of this everyday product. These include the transportation associated with: the production and supply of nitrogen, phosphorous and potassium fertilisers; pesticides; processing equipment; and farm machinery. It is likely that other ingredients such as sugar, vinegar, spices and salt were also imported. Most of the processes listed above will also depend on derivatives of fossil fuels. This product is also likely to be purchased in a shopping trip by car.

Food production is going to be an enormous problem in the Long Emergency. As industrial agriculture fails due to a scarcity of oil- and gas-based inputs, we will certainly have to grow more of our food closer to where we live, and do it on a smaller scale.

The priority must be the development of local and regional food systems, preferably organically based, in which a large percentage of demand is met within the locality or region. This approach, combined with fair trade, will ensure secure food supplies, minimise fossil fuel consumption and reduce the vulnerability associated with a dependency on food exports (as well as imports). Localising the food system will require significant diversification, research, investment and support that have, so far, not been forthcoming. But it is achievable and we have little choice.

Global Food Crisis And Starvation - Multinationals Making Billions

Giant agribusinesses are enjoying soaring earnings and profits out of the world food crisis which is driving millions of people towards starvation.

The prices of wheat, corn and rice have soared over the past two years driving the world's poor – who already spend about 80 per cent of their income on food – into hunger and destitution.

The World Bank in a report in May 2008 says that 100 million more people are facing severe hunger. Yet some of the world's richest food companies are making record profits. Monsanto in May 2008 reported that its net income for the three months up to the end of February that year had more than doubled over  the same period in 2007, from $543m to $1.12bn. Its profits increased from $1.44bn to $2.22bn.

Cargill's net earnings soared by 86 per cent from $553m to $1.030bn over the same three months. And Archer Daniels Midland, one of the world's largest agricultural processors of soy, corn and wheat, increased its net earnings by 42 per cent in the first three months of 2008 from $363m to $517m. The operating profit of its grains merchandising and handling operations jumped 16-fold from $21m to $341m.

Similarly, the Mosaic Company, one of the world's largest fertiliser companies, saw its income for the three months ending 29 February 2008 rise more than 12-fold, from $42.2m to $520.8m, on the back of a shortage of fertiliser. The prices of some kinds of fertiliser have more than tripled over the past year as demand has outstripped supply. As a result, plans to increase harvests in developing countries have been hit hard.

The Food and Agriculture Organisation reported that 37 developing countries were in urgent need of food. Food riots broke out across the globe from Bangladesh to Burkina Faso, from China to Cameroon, and from Uzbekistan to the United Arab Emirates.

Benedict Southworth, director of the World Development Movement, called the escalating earnings and profits "immoral". He said that the benefits of the food price increases were being kept by the big companies, and were not finding their way down to farmers in the developing world.

The soaring prices of food and fertilisers mainly come from increased demand. This has partly been caused by the boom in biofuels, which require vast amounts of grain, but even more by increasing appetites for meat, especially in India and China; producing 1lb of beef in a feedlot, for example, takes 7lbs of grain.

World food stocks at record lows, export bans and a drought in Australia have contributed to the crisis, but experts are also fingering food speculation.

There was also outrage over multinational companies following disclosures in the same year that Shell and BP between them recorded profits of £14bn in the first three months of the year – or £3m an hour

– on the back of rising oil prices.

Death of Soil Is Death of Civilization

We have totally damaged our soil. The diesel power of tractors is much faster but it kills the soil. Food can only be grown by adding chemical fertilisers of nitrogen, phosphate and potassium. Majority of all food grown today is totally reliant on synthetic fertilisers. Without it

we would be in serious trouble. We have used fossil fuel to grow plants in soil that is otherwise dead and this works as long as we have the cheap fossil fuel to make the fertiliser and transport all the inputs and so on. But in the end when we don't have cheap fossil fuels we are going to need living soils once again

and that living soil is something that requires time and care

Bad soil is bad for global health, and the evidence is mounting that the world' soil is in trouble. We're dead without good soil. Soil holds minerals and organic compounds critical to life. Without good soil we have got nothing.

All over the world, more than seven and a half million acres of soil has been degraded. That's larger than the U.S. and Canada combined. What remains is ailing as a result of compaction, erosion and salination making it near impossible to plant and adding to greenhouse gases and air pollution. Soil degradation is putting the future of the global population is at risk according to a National Geographic article by Charles Mann.

Civil unrest in Latin America, Asia and Africa have been attributed to a lack of food and affordable food as a result of poor soil. *Currently, only 11-percent of the world's land feeds six billion people.*

Experts estimate that by 2030 the Earth's population will reach 8.3 billion. Farmers will need to increase food production by 40-percent. But not much soil remains.

Scientists don't know much and don't care either about this critical resource.

Many organic farmers are reviving age old practices of cow dung fertilizers and cow urine pesticides. Popularly known as 'zero-budget farming', it is being practiced on thousands of acres across India with great success. When nourished by mother cow, soil remains fertile for thousands and millions of years but when scorched by chemicals, it dies in 3-4 decades.

Cows eat our leftovers. We take the grains and stem and grass is used for the cows. Similarly chaff and oil cakes feed the cows. There is perfect cooperation in nature's plan. We feed the cow with these byproducts and cow in turn feeds our crops.

In an experiment at the Dairy Research Institute, Ellinbank, Victoria, effects of dairy cow manure on soil fertility was observed. In the soil, extractable soil P (Olsen) was 32mg/kg. After 60 days of application, extractable soil P increased to 61mg/kg. Extractable soil K (Colwell) almost doubled from 642 mg/kg to 1226 mg/kg in manure treated soils.

Cows return significant quantities of nutrients to pastures through dung and urine. Up to 65% of the phosphorus (P) eaten in the diet is returned in faeces while approximately 11% and 79% of the consumed potassium (K) is returned in dung and urine respectively (Haynes and Williams, 1993). These nutrients contribute to soil fertility.

In another experiment in Kerala, India, a manure prepared with fermented cow dung, enriched with groundnut cake and neem cake was effective in improving soil quality and enhancing microbial status. In this State famous for black pepper farming, black pepper often suffers from poor growth and wilt disease. This has been linked to the intensive application of chemicals that has led to imbalances in soil micro-flora and fauna and resulted in the spread of diseases like quick wilt and slow wilt which are caused by soil born pathogens. These problems can be alleviated by improving soil fertility and soil microbial status using fermented cow dung enriched with groundnut cake and neem cake. Application of this manure to black pepper increases growth and improves soil status.

Farming In A Low-energy Future.

An approaching energy crisis will affect what we eat, where it comes from and even the alarming question of whether there will be enough food to keep us fed. If we are to survive we will have to change.

And it seems that the sooner we begin that transition to a new low energy future the easier the task will be.

Rwandan Agriculture Growing – One Cow At A Time

Rwanda, a conflict torn fragile state of yesteryears is boasting of peace and security, demonstrating food security and leading regionally in aid management and on governance issues. The reforms and efforts in the agriculture sector are a major part of this transformation. And behind this transformation of a nation stands the humble cow, munching grass and looking curious.

One of the most compelling stories has been that of the process of agricultural transformation. Agriculture is an unmovable cornerstone of Rwandan society. Eighty percent of the people

depend on the land for their livelihoods. The land scarcity and the fact that Rwanda has one of the highest population densities in Africa, culminate in farming being conducted by smallholders who own, on average, 0.5 hectares of farmland.

'With a high population density and a lack of cultivatable unoccupied land, farmer productivity increases are paramount. With this in mind, the Ministry of Agriculture and Animal Resources designed the Crop Intensification Program. Parallel to the Crop Intensification program and equally as important in dealing with poverty, and definitely more powerful in dealing with malnutrition, is the One Cow per Poor Family Program—locally known as the *Girinka* Program.

'This program like many other initiatives in Rwanda has deep roots in the Rwanda culture: where malnutrition in kids is a shame to family

"The dairy cow has played a central role in improving Rwanda's household nutrition as well as agricultural productivity."
—*Agnes Kalibata, Minister for Agriculture, Rwanda*

and society and where sharing a cow (passing on an offspring to other families) builds very strong society bonds. The Girinka Program, started by the President in 2006, has secured a productive asset in the hands of poor farmers and mitigated child malnutrition with milk drinking. The program now targets about 350,000 poor families across the country of whom 92,000 have already received a cow. This program has locally been scored as most successful of all economic uplifting programs at the household level. The externalities are enormous; besides dealing with malnutrition, farmers have income from the sale of extra milk and offsprings from the cow, they access manure for their land—a factor that has seen crop and livestock very neatly integrated in Rwanda.

The most powerful externality however, is at the society level; a farmer who receives a cow passes on the first female offspring to another needy farmer. This has built a strong sense of community bonding that Rwanda needs very badly. Recently, the IFAD [International Fund for Agricultural Development] President was visiting farmers in Rwanda and one beneficiary of a cow from an IFAD supported project proudly showed him his bank book. The President asked him there was anything that IFAD could do to improve his life even more and the farmer said "Yes, give a cow to my neighbours who are still waiting their turn."

One Cow Per Family Programme is set to expand to reach those most in need over the next three years.

Cuba - The Lessons Learnt

Cows have a rich history in Cuba. Spanish conquistador Diego Velazquez, the former governor of Cuba, brought 970 cows to the island in the years 1512 to 1524. Their numbers multiplied. By the mid-1500s, cattle hide had replaced gold as the main currency of exchange in Cuba.

From then on, the cattle industry was the No. 1 source of income to the Cuban economy up to the end of the 18th century, From about 1800 until 1958, there was at least one cow for every person in Cuba.

After the revolution, the government confiscated all cattle farms larger than 66 acres. Sugar production became the priority and the number of cows dwindled.

The agriculture also took a plunge during the period and Cuba became a net food importer to feed its 11 million people.

Arturo Riera, president of the National Association of Cuban Cattlemen says, "Before the revolution, you could see cows all over, everything has changed. The number of cows has plunged from 6.3 million in 1958 to less than 2 million today. The regime did nothing to prevent the slaughter of countless head of cattle. Now they buy 50 cows from USA. That's not going to do a darn thing. You cannot improve an industry that had more than 6 million cows overnight. It will take years to restore the Cuban cattle industry to its former grandeur."

Golden Cows of Cuba - "I'm worth more than you"

But there has been an awakening in Cuba. Today the cows are sacred in Cuba. A colorful etching spotted at an Old Havana crafts market underscored that point, depicting a cow saying, "I'm worth more than you."

That's because a person can get more jail time for killing a cow than killing a human, under Cuban law. Cow killers can get four to 10 years in prison under a toughened crime law. Those who transport or sell the meat from an illegally slaughtered cow can get three to eight years. Providing beef at an unauthorized restaurant or workplace can fetch two to five years. And buying contraband beef is punishable by three months to one year in jail or a steep fine. Authorities also have the power to confiscate all or part of the property of anyone involved in black-market cattle dealings.

In contrast, the jail sentence for homicide is generally seven to 15 years, unless there are aggravating circumstances. Suspects involved in contract hits, kidnap-murders, sadistic or perverse killings, the murder of police officials and other acts can get from 15 years in jail to the death penalty.

A Cuban cow called Ubre Blanca holds the world record in milk production. In 1982, the cow produced 28 gallons of milk in a day, about four times more than average. Later, it produced 6,309 gallons in 305 days. Both are world records. The cow died in 1985. Meanwhile, the animal has been stuffed and is on display at Cuba's cattle institute.

Milk remains in short supply in Cuba and is rationed. Mothers with infants younger than 1 are allowed to buy containers of milk for about 2 cents, a heavily subsidized price. Families with pregnant women or children younger than 7 can buy 2.2-pound bags of powdered milk for less than 10 cents. All other Cubans pay the market price. A container of milk goes for $1.45.

Cuba is also taking lead in preparing for post-petroleum farming. In Cuba, the ox is mightier than the tractor. Ox is viewed as way to ramp up food production while conserving energy. Cuba may rely more heavily than ever on oxen to save fuel normally used by heavy machinery.

President Castro is promoting the draft animals as a way for the economically strapped communist country to ramp up food production while conserving energy. He recently suggested expanding a pilot program that gives private farmers fallow government land to cultivate - but without the use of gas-guzzling machinery.

"For this program we should forget about tractors and fuel, even if we had enough. The idea is to work basically with oxen," Castro told parliament on Aug. 1, 2009. "An increasing number of growers have been doing exactly this with excellent results."

Though the island gets nearly 100,000 free barrels of oil a day from Venezuela, it also has begun a campaign to conserve crude. The agricultural ministry in late June proposed increasing the use of oxen to save fuel. The ministry said it had more than 265,000 oxen "capable of matching, and in some cases overtaking, machines in labor load and planting."

In the farming initiative that began last year, about 82,000 applicants have received more than 1.7 million acres so far — or 40 percent of the government's formerly idle land. Shortages in Cuba are not new. And neither are oxen. Thousands of Cuban farmers have relied on the beasts in the half century since Fidel and Raul Castro took over the country. "The ox means so much to us. Without oxen, farming is not farming," says Omar Andalio, 37, as he carefully coaxes a pair of government-owned beasts through a sugarcane field.

India - Cow Killing And Death of A Great Civilization

India of yore is examplified by Vrindavan, an ancient pastoral village. Vrindavan is a typical representation of Vedic India, an India that was known all over the world for her immense wealth and a highly advanced culture. Cows formed the backbone of it and cows were such an inseparable part of its daily life that Indian culture can safely be termed as cow culture.

When the British colonized India, they studied India thoroughly to keep her under subjugation. The then Governor of British India, Robert Clive made an extensive research in Indian economic and agricultural systems. He found that Indian society was firmly footed in its age-old customs and sound economic and agricultural practices, all based on cow protection. We can quote a letter of Lord MCLau here, a British colonial dated February 2, 1835.

> "I have traveled across the length and breath of India and I have not seen one person who is a beggar, who is a thief, such wealth I have seen in this country, such high moral values, people of such caliber (of noble character), that I do not think we would ever conquer this country...........unless we break the very backbone of this nation which is her spiritual and cultural heritage."

So during his surveys, Robert Clive found that in 1740, in the Arcot District of Tamil Nadu, 54 Quintals of rice was harvested from one acre of land using manure and pesticides made from cow urine and cow dung. Cow was the foundation of this great nation and cows greatly outnumbered men. He realized that unless this foundation was shaken up, they could not keep their hold on India for too long. This inspired him to open the first ever slaughterhouse in Indian in 1760, with a capacity to kill thousands of cows every week. As a part of the master plan to destabilize India, cow slaughter was initiated. To this extent, the British were quite successful. Cow slaughter, engineered by them, divided Hindu and Muslim communities which had coexisted peacefully for the last 700 years. Millions died in ensuing riots which lasted for decades. To this day, India and Pakistan are locked in bitter enemity and are continuously suffering.

Robert Clive started a number of slaughter houses before he left India. By 1910, 350 slaughterhouses were working day and night. India was reduced to severe poverty, millions were dying from hunger and malnutrition, age-old cottage industries were devastated and village artisans took up jobs as coolies in cities. Manchester cloth effectively destroyed Indian handlooms and textiles enterprise. Using Indian money and Indian man power, the British were expanding their empire all over the world.

Bereft of its cattle wealth, India had to approach England for industrial manure. Thus industrial manure like urea and phosphate made way to India. Indian villages, in which once flowed streams of milk and butter, became haunted hamlets, wretched and starving. A Paradise was lost. An India where horses and bullocks were made to drink ghee, was now suffering from scarcity of margarine. It was total devastation of a great civilization.

The British established an educational system which decried anything connected with Indian tradition. This was a crafty engineering by Macaulay who said, "We must at present do our best to form a class of persons Indian in blood and colour but English in tastes, in opinion, in morals, and in intellect." He did this so effectively that even after sixty years of independence Indians still continue to exist in a state of stupor, unable (and even unwilling!) to extricate themselves from one of the greatest hypnoses woven over a whole nation.

So by the time British departed from India, thousands of slaughterhouses were in operation and now after independence, its hard to keep a count of them. Instead of there being improvement in the well-being of the cow and reduction in the cow slaughter, as was expected after the departure of the British from India in 1947, the suffering, decline and ill-treatment of the cow multiplied manyfold. A large responsibility for this state of affairs falls on the post-1950 policies of the Government of India.

The result - 40000 suicides by Indian farmers every year, failing agriculture and highest number of malnourished children in the world.

Indian government is proud of the fact that India today is the third largest beef exporter in the world. It is introducing factory farming in a big way and is completely oblivious of the fact that conditions in Western countries and India greatly differ and what may work there for sometime will not work here at all.

29.

Recipe To Save The Planet

One Old Man And A Bucket Of Cow Dung

Can one man with a bucket of cow dung be a recipe to save the planet? No claim could be more preposterous and more insane. Thats until you watch the international awards winning film, One Man One Cow One Planet. This is a story of a New Zealander spearheading a silent revolution in some of the world's most destitute areas, all alone with a bucket of cow dung. This film is being claimed to be a blueprint for a post-industrial future. It takes you into the heart of the world's most important renaissance.

Hero of the film, Peter Proctar is an eighty year old gardener and soil expert from New Zealand. He comes with a vast experience of sixty years in his field.

His favourite animal is the cow because of all the dung it provides. Dung is something that Proctor prizes more highly than gold, jewels, fossil fuels, or many other natural resources. His favourite invertebrate is the earthworm, which he describes as "the unpaid servant of soil health."

In the film, his farm operates on human scale, and is self sustaining, ethical and biologically diverse. It is a blue print for future when fossil fuels will be scarce. World's most valuable commodity will be the knowledge of how to farm and the wisdom of how to grow food that is more than just stuff to fill our stomachs. Indeed what he is presenting may be the last chance this planet has.

His proposal assumes significance as our existence on this planet gets precarious and as modern industrial agriculture destroys the earth.

Desertification, water scarcity, toxic cocktails of agricultural chemicals are pervading our food chains as ocean ecosystems collapse and soil erosion and massive loss of soil fertility take place all over the world. Our ecosystems ore overwhelmed. Humanity's increasing demands are exceeding the Earth's carrying capacity. Modern agriculture causes topsoil to be eroded at 3 million tons per hour. (that's 26 billion tons a year)

Human mass is replacing biomass and other species. The carrying capacity of the earth is almost spent. To maintain our comfort zone lifestyles we will soon need five earths to sustain us in the style to which we have become accustomed.

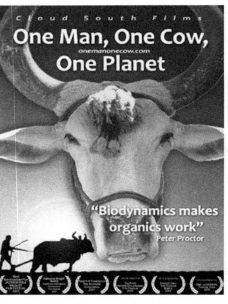

Mainstay of any civilization is its agriculture. It thrives and survives on agriculture, because food is all that matters, first and foremost. Two other essential ingredients, water and air are of course free. Industries are artificial and they sap the vitality of human beings and nature. They deplete all resources, human, environmental and natural. Industries are a short run drama and a drama doesn't last very long. Next few decades will see the sad ending of this drama when the curtain of realities falls. Agriculture is real life. Drama is for few hours and real life is forever.

Modern industrial agriculture is a form of molesting earth. Humanity is set to pay a big price for this callousness, for this crime. Lesser and lesser number of people today are having an interest in agriculture. Unscrupulous profit crazy corporations are taking over small farms. These corporations have only one relationship with Earth - that of exploitation & profiteering. All this can not last forever. We are taking food for granted, we are taking God's nature for granted. Its not going to work. Something has to change and something will change, whether we like it or not.

Agriculture is still the occupation of almost 50% of the world's population, but the numbers vary from less than 3% in industrialized countries to over 60% in Third World countries.

What if the world were an apple? One quarter of the apple is land and the rest is water. Cut the one quarter of apple, that is land, into half and put aside that half which is deserts and mountains. Peel of what is left and that represents the topsoil that must feed the whole world. This analogy illustrates how important it is to get the best out of the available soil to provide abundant and nutritious food for everyone on the planet.

But modern agriculture couldn't care less for this precious resource. Modern agriculture is at war. It is at war with the mother Earth, with the environment. The weapons used in this war are massive agricultural machines, chemical fertilizers, herbicides, fungicides, pesticides and now genetic manipulation of the crops.

At the end of World War II, military industrial complex needed new markets for its surplus chemicals. It gave birth to Agriculture Industrial Complex. Decades of our addiction to these chemicals have led to toxic oceans, toxic water, toxic air and toxic food. From chemical deserts of factor farms to our inner life, our world as a place of nature is unrecognizable.

Most of us are far removed from the fields where our food is grown. Separating us from our food, our primary source of life, is a vast globalized distribution system, controlled my multinational corporations.

Fight against corporate control of our food, is the fight for food sovereignty. When corporations dictate what farmers must grow, they are controlling what all of us must eat. The outcome of battle for agricultural control may dictate the future of the Earth.

India - A Case Study

Peter has been working with crisis-struck farmers in India for the past fifteen years and providing a strong grassroots alternative to industrialised conventional agriculture, which is failing on all counts.

India was one of the richest countries in the world, not because of its gold, diamonds or rubies, but because of its bio-mass. In India they could grow anything because of wonderful temperature, wonderful climate, the moisture and the warmth. That was the secret of India's legendary wealth.

India has been an agro-based economy since time immemorial. Cow has been an integral part (backbone) of its agriculture. But during industrial development and Green revolution, they switched over to chemical based and machine based farming, replacing age old methods involving cow dung, cow urine, and bull power. Today chemical-based farming (Green Revolution) has rewarded India with degradation of soil, low yields of crops, emergence of new pests and diseases and percolation of toxic chemicals into the food chain. This has resulted in more than 1.85 lakh farmers committing suicide all over India in last 15 years. For millennia, organic cow based farming was practiced in India without any marked decline in soil fertility.

Green revolution was supposed to alleviate India's hunger. Viewed

We know when India was more primitive, there were thousands of cows owned by the agriculturists and they used to enjoy life by the agricultural products and sufficient quantity of clarified butter, milk and curd. Even some hundreds of years before during the reign of Nawab Swaesta Khan, rice was selling in India at the rate of nine mounds (40kg) a rupee and today ever since the beginning of scientific knowledge in India, rice is selling now at the rate of nine chatak (60gms) a rupee. In the former days, the Indian kings and rich men used to perform yajnas by burning tons and tons of pure clarified butter made out of cow's milk and at the present moment there is not a drop of pure clarified butter made out of cow's milk even for daily use. That is the law of material nature. Leaving aside the stories of Nawab Sawesta Khan's history we can say from our personal experience that my father say 40 years before at most used to stock at our house (in Calcutta) always a cart load of rice, 15 mounds (40kg), ten seers (1kg) of pure ghee, a bag of potato and a cart load of soft coke always ready for use. Our family was not a rich family and my father's income was within Rs. 250/- per month. And it was within his easy reach to stock household provisions in the above manner. But at the present moment at no house in the cities and towns generally there is stock of more than 15 seers (1kg) of rice. Formerly they used to enquire rates of commodities in the terms of mounds (40kg) and now they ask for it in terms of seers (1kg) or chattacks (60gms) although we are able to keep more glittering cars than cows at the present moment.
— *Srila Prabhupada (Back To Godhead magazine, Nov. 1956)*

holistically, green revolution was a failure. Chemical agriculture destroyed India's natural abundance, farming communities and soil. High yielding plant varieties turned out to use far more water, growing significantly less crop per drop. Today in much of India, rivers have long since dried up. The only water is hundreds of meters down.

Just the thirty or forty years of chemical usage has destroyed the soil which was working flawlessly since thousands of years. International Water Management Institute describes India's green revolution as 'living on borrowed water, and borrowed time'.

As an alternative to this destruction, the method Peter Proctar is proposing is called biodynamic farming. Cow which is venerated in India, is central to this biodynamic farming. With her 4 stomach, she is a unique animal of digestion. Cow dung forms the basis of many biodynamic preparations. Cow Pat Pit (CPP) is one way of processing cow dung. Proctors call is 'Muck And Magic' because the recipe contains mystical preparations.

A farmer who acquired a field six years ago was asked - how was the land when you started? He replied, "It was quite hard, like a rock." Why? "Because they were using chemicals at that time." How is it now? "In last six years, I have put compost and green manure, and it has become like cotton and even further it has become like butter. Its so smooth and easy to cultivate." Why are so many birds here while you are cultivating. "There is such a population of earth worms now, and as I cultivate they eat the earthworms and insects as they come out," came the reply. Healthy soil makes healthy plants, healthy animals and healthy people.

Cow Based Biodynamic Agriculture

Biodynamic agriculture is an advanced form of organic agriculture with an emphasis on food quality and soil health ; and as such, uses no synthetic fertilizers or pesticides. 'Biodynamic' originates from two Greek words, *bios* meaning life, and *dynamos* meaning energy. The pioneer of biodynamic agriculture was Rudolf Steiner (1861-1925) an Austrian scientist, philosopher, and educator. He identified the deleterious effects on the soil and the deterioration of the health and quality of crops and livestock that farmers experienced following the introduction of chemical fertilizers at the turn of the twentieth century. In a series of eight lectures known as the "*Agricultural Course*" made in 1924 Steiner taught the fundamental ecological principle that the farm is a living organism, an individual self-contained entity within a whole harmonious system. Bio-dynamics is a complete holistic outlook on agriculture. Though the Steiner theory of biodynamics might be a bit esoteric on reading, when it is put into practice, it becomes eminently practical.

Bio-dynamic agriculture is the oldest organic farming movement practiced in over 40 countries in the world. It includes the normal organic farming practices, such as the use of compost, green manures, and crop rotation. In addition, Bio-dynamic agriculture uses a series of Preparations numbered from 500 to 508 which are based on various mineral, plant, and animal substances. These enhance all the bacterial, fungal and mineral processes that are found in the organic farming system. Placing great importance on the auspicious positions of the moon, sun

and planets, a Planting Calendar is used for applying the biodynamic preparations, sowing seeds, planting plants, applying liquid manures, spraying fruit trees and crops, and other farming activities. Experience has shown that use of the Bio-dynamic techniques can make all organic farming processes work more quickly and better.

A biodynamic farm is characterized by self-sufficiency and biological diversity where crops and livestock are integrated, nutrients are recycled, and the health of the soil, the crops and animals, and the farmer too, are maintained holistically. Consideration of the farm as an ecosystem feeds into holistic management practices that embrace the environmental, social and economic aspects of the farm.

Its objectives differ significantly from those of conventional agriculture, or agribusiness, which maximizes profit with mechanical and technological inputs for unlimited exploitation of the earth's resources.

Dr. Patel: They have in Bengal this Standard Pharmaceuticals of Bengal, been able to isolate penicillin from cow dung, and they have a big plant in Calcutta producing penicillin from cow dung. It's stated, you know, how cow dung was considered sacred. Perhaps we did not know that, but by experience.

Prabhupäda: Before this, one Monmohan Gosh, Dr. Monmohan Gosh, he was pathologist in medical college. He proved the antiseptic properties of cow dung. He was Dr. Gosh's friend. So he was working in his laboratory also. I know. Long ago.

Dr. Patel: And in cow urine, sir, there are so many hormones coming, and a big sample of hormones which can be resynthesized as human hormones. That is why gomutra is being drunk.

Prabhupäda: Gomutra is good medicine for liver disease. If you drink urine of...

Dr. Patel: Yes, it is proved scientifically so many hormones and by-products and hormones which can be resynthesized into human hormones, modern science.

Dr. Patel: That's right, cow urine is considered sacred by we people that we put a drop in the newly born child's mouth.

Prabhupäda: Pancha-gavya, gomutra is one of the parts. Cow dung, urine, milk, yogurt, and ghee. This is pancha gavya, pertaining to the cow.

— Srila Prabhupada (Morning Walk — August 14, 1976, Bombay)

The biodynamic model feeds family and farm workers first, and then trade surpluses to the local community. One main difference between organic and biodynamic farms is that organic farms often exclude animals for ethical reasons and monocrop production is common.

Movements like this may be the last chance this planet has for a healthy, secure, and ecologically efficient food supply.

An Emergent Agricultural Knowledge System Against The Corporate Takeover

Biodynamic farms have broad ecological implications as a blueprint for agriculture when fossil fuels are scarce But they have cultural implications too. Today in India, biodynamic and organic farming methods represent a revolution, one farmer at a time, against the vested interests of agribusiness disguised as science and the global dominance of corporations such as Monsanto.

The advantage of a cow based biodynamic farming for Indian farmers is that they are practising a form of non-chemical, non-toxic farming that does not require the use of any hybrid or GM seeds. Monsanto is a company thats trying to monopolise seed production and its only objective is that every farmer in the world who buys seed should buy from Monsanto. As 60 percent of India's population depends on small and marginal farming, the impact of stopping traditional methods of seed saving and swapping, and taking farmers to court for patent

infringement where they are fined 1-2 million rupees, is literally killing them. Indian farmers want freedom and independence from corporate control. They don't want any Monsanto or Syngenta to tell us what seed they grow and what crop they should harvest and what food to eat. This perspective reflects Gandhi's definition of food sovereignty or the right of all people to decide what they grow and eat free of international market forces.

Peter Proctor's book, Grasp the Nettle explains how it all works. The cow dung is used to create compost and it has to be prepared in a particular way. It involves CPP or Cow Pat Pits where the cow dung is layered in pits. One preparation involves the dung being put into cow horns and then being buried. It is left in these pits right through winter after which the crumbly textured mix it turns into is mixed with water and sprayed on the crops. This preparation enables the plant to hold on the moisture for longer and helps the roots go deeper. The experiments are a total success – farms that have adopted this method have healthier and juicier crops. Little wonder that Peter Proctor is almost venerated by the rural Indian farmer, many of whom have wiped out their debts and shed the yoke of corporate control thanks to following his 'back to Nature' philosophy. When they hear he's visiting, they come from miles around, sitting around him with their ubiquitous cell phones, waiting to hear the words of wisdom that fall from his mouth about the state of

At least in India, say, hundred years before, there was no problem for eating, even for the lower class or any... No, there was no... The society was so made, there was no problem. Why fifty years? In 1933 or '36 in Vrndavana somebody wanted milk, some pilgrims amongst ourselves. So went to a house. "Can you supply us some milk?" "Ah, how much you want?" So it was about ten pounds. So she supplied immediately, one woman, and when she was offered price, "Oh, why shall I take a price for ten or twenty pounds of milk? Oh, you can take it." That is my practical experience. Milk was so freely available. So simply we are creating problems by godless civilization. That is a fact.
— Srila Prabhupada (Room Conversation, December 21, 1970, Surat, India)

the soil. After all, it's because of him that thousands of Indian farmers have stopped using chemical fertilizers and pesticides and have adopted biodynamics as a way of life.

Maybe it was easier in India than anywhere else in the world. After all, the cow has always been worshipped and it was easy enough to make them see why this way was so much better. Cow dung has

Prabhupada: Driving at breakneck speed. And then what is the business? Searching out some means of food, exactly like the hog, he is loitering here and there, "Where is stool? Where is stool? Where is stool?" And this is going on in the polished way as civilization. There is so much risk, as running these cars so many people are dying. There is record, it is very dangerous. At least I feel as soon as I go to the street, it is dangerous. The motorcar are running so speedy, and what is the business? The business is where to find out food. So therefore it is condemned that this kind of civilization is hoggish civilization. This hog is running after, "Where is stool? And you are running in a car. Purpose is the same: Therefore this is not advancement of civilization. Advancement of civilization is, as Krsna advises, that you require food, so produce food grain. Remain wherever you are. You can produce food grain anywhere, a little labor. And keep cows, go-raksya, krsi-go-raksya vanijyam vaisya-karma svabhava-jam [Bg. 18.44]. Solve your problem like... Produce your food wherever you are there. Till little, little labor, and you will get your whole year's food. And distribute the food to the animal, cow, and eat yourself. The cow will eat the refuse. You take the rice, and the skin you give to the cow. From dahl you take the grain, and the skin you give to the... And fruit, you take the fruit, and the skin you give to the cow, and he will give you milk. So why should you kill her? Milk is the miraculous food; therefore Krsna says cow protection. Give protection to the cow, take milk from it, and eat food grains -- your food problem is solved. Where is food problem? Why should you invent such civilization always full of anxieties, running the car here and there, and fight with other nation, and economic development? What is this civilization?
— Srila Prabhupada (Philosophical discussion)

traditionally had a number of uses in India – made into cakes and burnt as fuel, mixed with water and applied on floors to prevent insects from coming into the home and to manufacture biogas. And maybe the typical small holding Indian farmer was in tune with his land – and his cow of course – to realize that the so called green revolution, ushered in by the global pesticide manufacturers, only resulted in polluting the soil, poisoning it as well as the ground water. Unlike many other places in the world, the harsh effects of chemical farming were much more visible here much sooner. With over half the population in India depending on agriculture, this was devastating!

Maybe that's why Peter Proctor can be seen working among the rural farmers of India - maybe it was so much easier to convince people who lived in close communion with the land rather than farmers in more westernized societies where it takes much longer for the ill effects of chemical farming to be felt. Maybe when the holdings are small and so much depends on it, there's a sensitivity to the soil and its needs – and an awareness of when things are good and in harmony with the rest of nature.

India's Organic Farms Work At Village Level

During the past fifteen years, Peter Proctor has visited India twenty five times to teach biodynamic farming methods to as many farmers as possible. Despite his eighty years, he visits ten villages a day. Proctor's involvement is part of a major campaign to promote and encourage alternative forms of agriculture that use no synthetic inputs in response to an epidemic of farmer suicides, most of whom were farming GM crops. This initiative has encouraged 4 million hectares under organic farming methods and 1000 officially supported training schemes for biodynamic and organic farms in the Maharastra region, a suicide hotspot. These farms work at village level and each village has formed an organic federation accredited at district level where farmers participate to solve their own problems. By building up their knowledge base, farmers gain independence from agribusinesses through reducing external inputs. By using biological practices such as green manures, cover cropping, companion planting, and natural insecticides, money is saved that would have been spent on costly pesticides and fertilizers, and is put back into their own communities to improve the quality of life of everyone. This great change in rural prosperity has brought whole communities back together again and enabled the integration of health education in local settings.

The good news about the benefits of this cow based farming has spread quickly and there are now in excess of 2,00,000 compost piles

For the time being, if you actually want to develop such ideal asrama, we must have sufficient land, and all other things will gradually grow. For raising crops from the land, how many men will be required—that we must estimate and for herding the cows and feeding them. We must have sufficient pasturing ground to feed the animals all round. We have to maintain the animals throughout their life. We must not make any program for selling them to the slaughterhouses. That is the way of cow protection. Krishna by His practical example taught us to give all protection to the cows and that should be the main business of New Vrindaban. Vrindaban is also known as Gokula. Go means cows, and kula means congregation. Therefore the special feature of New Vrindaban will be cow protection, and by doing so, we shall not be loser. In India of course, a cow is protected and the cowherdsmen they derive sufficient profit by such protection. Cow dung is used as fuel. Cow dung dried in the sunshine kept in stock for utilizing them as fuel in the villages. They get wheat and other cereals produced from the field. There is milk and vegetables and the fuel is cow dung, and thus, they are self-independent in every village. There are hand weavers for the cloth. And the country oil-mill (consisting of a bull walking in circle round two big grinding stones, attached with yoke) grinds the oil seeds into oil. The whole idea is that people residing in New Vrindaban may not have to search out work outside. Arrangements should be such that the residents should be self-satisfied. That will make an ideal asrama. I do not know these ideals can be given practical shape, but I think like that; that people may be happy in any place with land and cow without endeavoring for so-called amenities of modern life—which simply increase anxieties for maintenance and proper equipment. The less we are anxious for maintaining our body and soul together, the more we become favorable for advancing in Krishna Consciousness.

—Srila Prabhupada (Letter to: Hayagriva, Montreal 14 June, 1968)

throughout India that recycles cow dung, paddy straw and almost anything else nature provides. Recycling local and freely available resources such as leaves and dung from the ubiquitous and revered cows provides an appropriate alternative technological strategy for Indian farmers and doesn't cost lives.

Alternatives To The "Green Revolution"

How to Save the World is an award winning independent film that documents the progress of Peter Proctor and his cow based biodynamic farming movement in India. Writer and director Barbara Burstyn treats us to visions of verdant biodynamic farms where colorfully dressed young

men and women prepare the field preparations and spray them in spiral motions from large copper bowls onto the soil. The old ploughman driving two golden cows tells his story of how the soil has become soft and almost butter-like and alive with worms under biodynamic systems. Elsewhere, we see vast areas of land where the soil is so saturated with layer upon layer of chemicals that it has become great lumps of dry, dusty boulders where no life exists. Organic farmer Jaspal Singh explains that this is the result of the "Green Revolution", that has not only been a killer of farmers, but has made the soil unproductive, waterlogged, pest infested, depleted of nutrients, and has dried up rivers. Singh says that until he learned about chemical free organic and biodynamic farming systems that uses fifty percent less water, he had no alternative to the chemical and water intensive practices of the Green Revolution.

Despite the negative effects of chemicals on the soil, the use of pesticides is increasing and claims the lives of at least 2,00,000 people per year in India by direct poisoning.

In India, seed dealers get huge commission from chemical companies and Indian farmers are forced to take hybrid seeds and pesticides as part of credit packages from salesmen in order to continue to farm. Shantytowns of farmers evicted from their lands because of failed harvests and unpaid debts have sprung up by the rows of pesticide sellers set up in small roadside huts with shelves filled with packets of GM seeds and cans of pesticides. These seeds cost farmers four hundred percent more and yield thirty percent less. A 2006 report shows that 60 percent of farmers using GM seed could not cover their investment, let alone feed their families.

The film, *How to Save the World* captures the rhythmical movement and vitality of India, but cannot resist a cynical take on the corporate model that builds a market by forcing once independent farmers into debt and dependence on international aid for the very same grains and legumes they once grew successfully. It puts the blame for dependency and for world hunger fairly and squarely on the shoulders of industrial agriculture, genetic engineering, military dominance and trade liberalization, and not on food scarcity. The failure of the globalised free market is starkly symbolized by miles of empty toll roads, built as an infrastructure for corporate agriculture that many farmers in India cannot afford, or do not want.

How to Save The World leaves us in no doubt that one would be fortunate to find oneself connected to an idyllic rural biodynamic farm where pay and conditions for workers and their families are fair, food is of the highest quality and plentiful, the local economy thrives, the farm shop is a sell out, and the farmer and the local community is happy and content. And there is no reason why million more small to medium sized farming communities everywhere could not enjoy the same good life.

What Peter Proctor is doing however, is starting a revolution – quietly and effectively at the grassroots level of agricultural India. Why did this man come all the way from New Zealand braving the heat and dust of rural India to start a movement that would take on the might of multinationals and their juggernaut on its way to control everything we eat and drink? Why would a man who is partially deaf, with one glass eye, an opera buff, who doesn't particularly like spicy Indian curry come halfway across the world to try and save debt-ridden Indian farmers from the clutches of corporations like Monsanto?

Because he cares. Yes, Peter Proctor cares – and this caring goes beyond the farmers and their plight. He cares about the planet and what we as humans are doing to denigrate it. He cares enough to say, 'Enough!' and to do his bit to work in tandem with Nature, not against it. He cares enough to want to try and bring back the beauty of balance that Nature should ideally have. To repair the delicate web of interdependence that all creatures in the world should be connected with.

30.

Cow Killing Economics
Versus

Cow Protection Economics

A Historical Preview

Most people throughout world history have eaten a largely a vegetarian diet. Relatively recently, in Europe and North America, where meat and animal products became affordable, diets centered around meats became widespread. In other parts of the world, plant-based diets remained more common.

Indians are derided for considering the cow to be sacred or holy. The terms 'holy cow' or 'sacred cow' are often indicative of India's superstitions or blind beliefs.

But Indians are not alone in considering the cows to be holy. Almost all traditional societies subscribe to this view. Its not true that cow slaughter has always been a basic feature of civilizations outside India. The ancient Egyptians prohibited cow slaughter. The Hebrews, among others, restricted it to religious sacrifices. Vegetarianism was advocated zealously by numerous philosophers and writers of ancient Greece and Rome. In the Roman Catholic church, it was practised monastically by Trappists and among Protestants more recently by Seventh-Day Adventists. In the pastoral communities of East Africa, slaughter of cattle is only allowed during rituals and ceremonies, that too very rarely. It is said about them:

They sing to them.

They give them names.

They shelter the young ones in their homes.

Without the herd, the tribe will die.

To The Masai, the cow is life.

Of course, it is true that India is perhaps the only country (other than Nepal) where cows are 'worshipped' by a large majority of the people and its slaughter tabooed on wholly religious grounds. But prohibition of cow slaughter is by no means peculiar to India and, even if it is not always supported by religious scriptures, it is upheld by sentiment and convention having almost the same kind of popular sanction and force.

Quoted below is an authoritative pronouncement on the subject from none other than Mao Tsetung of China: "Draught oxen are a treasure to the peasants. As it is practically a religious tenet that 'Those who slaughter in this life will themselves become cattle in the next', draught oxen must never be killed. Before coming to power, the peasants had no means of stopping the  slaughter of cattle except the religious taboo. Since the rise of the Peasant Associations, they have extended their jurisdiction even over cattle and have prohibited their slaughter in the cities. Of the six beef shops in the country town of Hsiangtan, five are now closed and the remaining one sells only the beef of sick or disabled cattle. Cattle slaughter is prohibited throughout the country of Hengshan. A peasant whose cow stumbled and broke a leg had to consult the Peasant Association before he dared kill it. When the Chamber of Commerce of ChuChow slaughtered a cow, the peasants went to the town to protest and the Chamber, besides paying a fine, had to let off firecrackers by way of apology."' (*Report of an Investigation into the Peasant Movement in Hunan*', "*Selected Works of Mao Tsetung*", *Volume I, Lawrence and Wishart, London, 1954, pp 5253.*)

These observations were made by Mao Tsetung in the context of the peasant uprising in Hunan in 1926-27.

One might ask how an avowed atheistic leader such as Mao Tsetung could have allowed himself to support a religious belief against killing oxen? Anthropologist Marvin Harris suggests that religious and ritual restrictions on cow slaughter and eating of cow flesh were not irrational laws but important tools for the welfare of society. The draft power or milk of the animal was too valuable to lose. And wasting pasture to feed many cows for slaughter would eventually have brought starvation.

The economic rationale of these attitudes towards cow, and of the religious sanctions with which they were supported, have been clearly perceived through the ages by persons with very different predilections. "Cattle", the Buddha is believed to have said, "are our friends just like parents and other relatives, for cultivation depends upon them. They give food, strength, freshness of complexion and happiness. Knowing this, Brahmins of old did not kill cattle" (Suttanipata, 2956). More recently, Mahatma Gandhi offered the same diagnosis when he observed: "Why the cow was selected for apotheosis is obvious to me. The cow was in India the best companion. She was the giver of plenty. Not only did she give milk bat she also made agriculture possible." Surprisingly, even Karl Marx who had no direct knowledge of the problems of agriculture in India and had to depend on other sources of information was sufficiently impressed by the phenomenon to make an extensive reference to it while discussing the problems of circulating and fixed capital in the second volume of "Das Kapital": "'While the farmer is starving, his cattle thrive. There had been considerable rain and the grass pasture was luxuriant. The Indian farmer will starve alongside of a fat ox. The percepts of superstition seem cruel for the individual, but they are preserving society; the preservation of the cattle secures the continuation of agriculture and thereby the sources of future subsistence and wealth. It may sound hard, but it is so: In India a man is easier replaced than an ox'. *("Return, East Indian. Madras and Orissa Famine Number 4", page 4.)* Compare with the preceding the statement of Manu Dharma Sestra, chapter 10: 'The sacrifice of life without any reward, for the purpose of preserving a Brahmana or a cow ....can secure the salvation of even a lowborn outcaste'.

Not only in the Third World, but even in pre-industrial Europe, cow eating was rather rare because raising cows was labor-intensive, requiring pastures and feed, and oxen and cows were much more valuable as draught animals and for producing milk. Meat was more expensive and therefore in the form of game was common only on the tables of the nobility.

Cereals remained the most important staples during the Middle Ages in Europe. Barley, oat and rye among the poor, and wheat for the governing classes, were eaten as bread, porridge, gruel and pasta. Fava beans and vegetables were important supplements to the cereal-based diet.

Milk was an important source of animal protein. It would mostly come from cows, but milk from goats and sheep was also used. Cheese was far more important as a foodstuff, especially for common people, and it has been suggested that it was, during many periods, the chief supplier of animal protein among the lower classes. Many varieties of cheese eaten today were available and well known in late medieval times. Cheese was used in cooking for pies and soups. Butter, another important dairy product, was in popular use in the regions of Northern Europe, the Low Countries and Southern Scandinavia. While most other regions used oil or lard as cooking fats, butter was the dominant cooking medium in these areas. Its production also allowed for a lucrative butter export from the 12th century onward.

It was only after the Black Death had eradicated up to half of the European population that meat became more common even for poorer people. The drastic reduction in many populated areas resulted in a labor shortage, meaning that wages shot up. It left vast areas of farmland untended, making them available for pasture and putting more meat on the market.

But the real change came with the Industrial Revolution which changed the availability, distribution and production of food like never before. The 19th century brought with it huge growth in towns (the population of New York multiplied 80 times between 1800 and 1900), and  expansion of roads and railways. Interestingly, this period also brought the first food adulteration. With a rapidly increasing population, the food industry had a difficult time dealing with shortages of materials and in an effort to keep costs down, bulked up food items with questionable fillers.

By the 1850's the expanding industrial society experienced the most radical influence on the type and quantity of food available – the railway system. Previously, items had been hauled by horse or oxen, but the amount they could carry was limited. The railways were fast and could carry huge loads. Railways started to bring in carcasses rather than live animals, along with other foods from the country.

Factory life forced people to change what they ate. Unlike the farmer, the factory worker couldn't go home to a lunch of lentil stew or porridge. Bread and meat were more convenient. So the factory worker's food preference changed to meat, and because his income was increasing, he could afford it.

In The Industrial Revolution, Frederick Dietz writes, "Since meat was coming to be more valuable than powers of draft in an ox," traditional breeds that provided milk and draft power tended to be "replaced by such new breeds of cattle as the Durham shorthorns, the Herefords, and the Devons." So the industrial revolution bred beef cattle.

Creating Mass Consumption of Beef

So how did beef consumption increase so much?

According to Richard Robbins, the answers involve understanding the relationships among Spanish cattle, British colonialism, the American government, the American bison, indigenous peoples, the automobile, the hamburger, and the fast-food restaurant.

To summarize his detailed account:

As Spanish colonization of the Americas took hold, cattle were introduced in places like Argentina, Central America etc. By the seventeenth century cattle was so abundant, that one could be killed for the hide and the remaining meat left to rot.

Around the Industrial Revolution, England was the "beef-eating capital of the world." Not only to increase food for a growing population, but also to keep wages down, and due to the influence of wealthy meat

The economic development requires cow protections, but these rascals do not know. Their economic development' is cow killing. Just see, rascal civilization. Don't be sorry. It is sastra.

Therefore kurute vikarma. Simply for little satisfaction of the tongue, the same benefit you can derive from the milk, but because they are rascals, madmen, they think that eating or drinking the blood of the cow is better than drinking milk.

— Srila Prabhupada (Lecture, Srimad Bhagavatam, September 9, 1973)

industry leaders and landowners, beef consumption was made affordable to more and more people. The British Empire distributed much rum and meat to its military forces, thus helping to subsidize the sugar and meat industries.

To support an increasing demand, Britain would look to its empire, its colonies and other areas for additional beef and support of grain production. American meat industries, eager to make profits from the British demand looked to increase their cattle production.

However, they had to overcome problems including available rangeland

 and meeting the specific taste requirements of the British which, involved having fatter cows. But Indians and buffalo were in the lands that cattle producers needed for rangeland.

Hence, this led to the famous near extermination of the bison, which would also "deal" with the Indian problem. From just 1870 to 1880, millions of buffalo were reduced to "virtual extinction."

(The famous Buffalo Bill and others profited from hunting expeditions.)

This destroyed the Indians of the Plains, to whom buffalo were central in their culture as both a major food source and a life support system. They were moved off to reservations and other lands with no hope of continued meaningful existence.

To meet demands of fatty beef by the British, corn was increasingly fed to cattle. Furthermore, the price of grain was so cheap, it was advantageous to feed corn to cows. Thus, this formed a symbiotic relationship to the extent that even today the price of corn is closely linked to the demand for the price of cattle.

After World War II, the surge in automobile use led to the growth of the suburbs and fast-food restaurants that were making beef, and in particular, the hamburger a prime choice. Fast food and beef industries promoted each other.

Post World War II has seen "globalization" and consumption of fast foods such as McDonald's spread around the world, not just to the relatively wealthier West, but even in wealthy parts of the developing world. The fast-food restaurant, made possible by the popularity of the automobile, put the final touch on the ascendancy of beef.

Global demand for meat has multiplied in recent years, encouraged by growing affluence and nourished by the proliferation of huge, confined animal feeding operations. These assembly-line meat factories consume enormous amounts of energy, pollute water supplies, generate significant greenhouse gases and require ever-increasing amounts of corn, soy and other grains, a dependency that has led to the destruction of vast swaths of the world's tropical rain forests.

But this beef - cheap, plentiful, widely enjoyed and a part of daily life - may not be so forever. End of cheap oil and subsequent demise of industrial agriculture and cheap transport, will in turn end this two hundred years old saga of cheap beef. In the upcoming low energy future, if the world turns to ox power, beef may disappear from our dinner plates altogether. Sooner or later, we would have to make a transition from cow killing economics to a cow protection economics.

This cow killing economics is killing us in many ways. Dr. Neal Barnard says, "The beef industry has contributed to more American deaths than all the wars of this century, all natural disasters, and all automobile accidents combined. If beef is your idea of "real food for real people", you"d better live real close to a real good hospital."

31.

One Stop Solution

To All Economic Problems

By Srila Prabhupada

Money is required for purchasing food, but the animals, they do not know that food can be purchased. They are searching after food. But we are civilized; we are searching after money. Money is required for purchasing food. Why don't you produce food directly? That is intelligence. You are getting money, very good. What is that money? A paper. You are being cheated. It is written there, "hundred dollars." But what is that hundred dollars? It is cheap of..., piece of paper only. But because we are so fool, we are accepting a piece of paper, hundred dollars, and the struggle for existence for a piece of paper. Why don't you be intelligent — "Why shall I take the piece of paper? Give me food"? But

that intelligence you have lost. Therefore my Guru Maharaja used to say the present human society is combination of cheaters and cheated, that's all. No intelligent person. Formerly money was gold and silver coins. It had some value. But what is the present currency? Simply

 *"The gigantic industrial enterprises are products of a godless civilization." Godless civilization, they no more can depend on the natural gifts. They think by industrial enterprises, they will get more money and they'll be happy. And to remain satisfied with the food grains, vegetables and natural gifts, that is primitive idea. They say, "It is primitive."*

When men were not civilized, they would depend on nature, but when they are advanced in civilization, they must discover industrial enterprises.

They do not know what is spiritual life, what is ultimate goal. Simply like cats and dogs. The dog jumps over with four legs, and if a man can jump over with four wheels, then that is advance. Just see. They think, "Now we are advanced. We have got four-wheel car to jump over. And the dog is jumping with legs. Therefore this is advanced." They do not know this is also the same dog's business. They do not know it. [break] ...again they have made this car, coming from miles away, but the business is fishing. Just see. Bambharambhe laghu-kriya. "Advancement of civilization, we have got car, we are nicely dressed, we are human being, ev..." But what is your business? Fishing. Bambharambhe... Arambha, gorgeous arrangement — the business is the same. The skylark, what is called? Skylark? These birds?

Devotee (1): Oh, the seagulls. Seagull.

Prabhupada: Oh, seagull. They are doing the same business, and after his much advancement of civilization, he is doing the same business. The tiger is also eating flesh and blood, and human being — a scientific slaughterhouse. The same business, but they have got scientific instrument how to cut the throat quickly. This is the advance, advancement of civilization. The dog and cat they are having sex on the open street, and now they are talking of homosex in the school, colleges for education. This is their position. They do not know even what is the standard of human civilization. If you are doing the same business like ordinary animals, then where is the advancement of civilization?

—Srila Prabhupada (Lecture, Srimad-Bhagavatam, Mayapura, October 20, 1974)

piece of paper. Bunch of papers. During the last war the government failed in Germany, and these bunch of papers were thrown in the street. Nobody was caring. Nobody was caring.

So our civilization is based on that way. You require food. That's fact. Therefore Krsna says, *annad bhavanti bhutani* [Bg. 3.14]. You produce your food. Anywhere you can produce your food. There is enough land. In Australia you have got enough land. In Africa you have enough land, uncultivated. No. They'll not produce food. They will produce coffee and tea and slaughter animals. This is their business. I understand that in your country animals are slaughtered and exported for trade. Why export? You produce your own food and be satisfied. Why you are after that piece of hundred dollars paper? Produce your own food and eat sumptuously, be healthy and chant Hare Krsna. This is civilization. This is civilization. *(Lecture, Bhagavad-gita 9.4 — Melbourne, April 22, 1976)*

THE AUTHOR

Dr. Sahadeva dasa (Sanjay Shah) is a monk in vaisnava tradition. Coming from a prominent family of Rajasthan, he graduated in commerce from St.Xaviers College, Kolkata and then went on to complete his CA (Chartered Accountancy) and ICWA (Cost and works Accountancy) with national ranks. Later he received his doctorate.

For close to last two decades, he is leading a monk's life and he has made serving God and humanity as his life's mission. He has been serving as the president of ISKCON Secunderabad center since last twenty years.

His areas of work include research in Vedic and contemporary thought, Corporate and educational training, social work and counselling, travelling in India and aborad, writing books and of course, practicing spiritual life and spreading awareness about the same.

He is also an accomplished musician, composer, singer, instruments player and sound engineer. He has more than a dozen albums to his credit so far. (SoulMelodies.com) His varied interests include alternative holistic living, Vedic studies, social criticism, environment, linguistics, history, art & crafts, nature studies, web technologies etc.

His earlier books, Oil - A Global Crisis and Its Solutions (oilCrisisSolutions.com), End of Modern Civilization and Alternative future (WorldCrisisSolutions.com) have been acclaimed internationally.

OTHER BOOKS BY THE AUTHOR

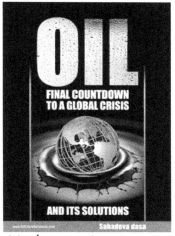

This unique book by the author examines the lifeline of modern living - petroleum. In our veins today, what flows is petroleum. Every aspect of our life, from food to transport to housing, its all petroleum based. Either its petroleum or its nothing. Our existence is draped in layers of petroleum. This book is a bible on the subject and covers every conceivable aspect of it, from its strategic importance to future prospects. Then the book goes on to delineate important strategic solutions to an unprecedented crisis thats coming our way.

Pages-330, www.OilCrisisSolutions.com

For a copy, write to: soulscienceuniversity@gmail.com

This book by Dr Sahadeva dasa is an authoritative work in civilizational studies as it relates to our future. Dr. Dasa studied human civilizations of last 5000 years and the reasons these civilizations went into oblivion. Each of these civilizations collapsed due to presence of one or two factors like neglect of soil, moral degradation, leadership crisis etc. But in our present civilization, all the factors that brought down all the these civilizations are operational with many more additional ones. Then the book goes on to chalk out the alternative future for mankind.

Pages-440, www.WorldCrisisSolutions.com

For a copy, write to: soulscienceuniversity@gmail.com

This landmark book on cow protection delineates various aspects of cow sciences as presented by the timeless voice of an old civilization, Vedas. This book goes on to prove that the cow will be the making or breaking point for humanity, however strange it may sound. Science of cow protection needs to be researched further and more attention needs to be given to this area. Most of the challenges staring in the face of mankind can be traced to our neglect in this area.

Pages-136,   Price-Rs100/-

www.cowism.com

For a copy, write to: soulscienceuniversity@gmail.com

This book discusses the vital role of cows in peace and progress of human society. Among other things, it also addresses the modern ecological concerns. It emphasizes the point that 'eCOWlogy' is the original God made ecology. For all the challenges facing mankind today, mother cow stands out as the single answer.

Living with cow is living on nature's income instead of squandering her capital. In the universal scheme of creation, fate of humans has been attached to that cows, to an absolute and overwhelming degree.

Pages-144,   Price-Rs100/-

www.cowism.com

For a copy, write to: soulscienceuniversity@gmail.com

This book deals with the internal lives of the cows and contains true stories from around the world. Cow is a very sober animal and does not wag its tail as often as a dog. This does not mean dog is good and cow is food. All animals including the dog should be shown love and care. But cow especially has a serious significance for human existence in this world. Talk about cows' feelings is often brushed off as fluffy and sentimental but this book proves it otherwise.

Pages 136, www.cowism.com

For a copy, write to: soulscienceuniversity@gmail.com

Music Albums: Download For Free From
Soul Melodies.com

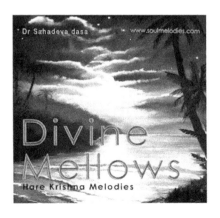

Music Albums: Download For Free From
Soul Melodies.com

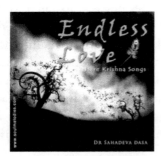

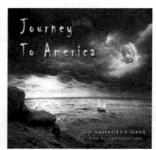